HOW TO SAVE AMERICA IN 10 EASY STEPS

JON FAVREAU ★ JON LOVETT ★ TOMMY VIETOR
WITH JOSH HALLOWAY

Crooked Media Reads

A zando IMPRINT

NEW YORK

Crooked Media Reads

Crooked Media Reads is an imprint of Zando.
zandoprojects.com

First Edition: June 2024

Cover design by Ramzy Masri
Text design by Sarah Schneider

The publisher does not have control over and is not responsible for author or
other third-party websites (or their content).

Library of Congress Control Number: 2023948986

978-1-63893-143-0 (Hardcover)
978-1-63893-185-0 (Signed edition)
978-1-63893-144-7 (ebook)

Manufactured in the United States of America
10 9 8 7 6 5 4 3 2 1

CONTENTS

PREAMBLE

GREETINGS, FELLOW CITIZEN! We're writing to you ahead of what is likely to be yet another scorcher of an election at a crucial moment for our country, while also having no idea where or when you are reading this. Maybe Greenland's ice shelf slid into the sea and you live on a floating barge city where protein is your currency. Maybe you've pulled the charred remains of this guide from a book burning in Daytona Beach, which is now our nation's capital. Or maybe . . . just maybe . . . everything is totally great?!

But probably not. More likely, you just saw a news alert on your phone or ad-supported retina display and now your stomach hurts. We know how easy it is to be overwhelmed by politics and underwhelmed by politicians. The three of us ~~wasted~~ spent our formative and hottest years in politics. We each cut our teeth working on some presidential campaigns that didn't quite pan out: Favreau for John Kerry, Lovett for Hillary Clinton, and Tommy for John Edwards (before the sex stuff). Eventually, we all worked in the White House together for Barack Obama, where we wrote speeches (Favreau and Lovett), shaped press coverage on national security issues (Tommy), and performed secret gay weddings in the Rose Garden (keep reading to find out!). After totally solving Washington's most pressing problems, we left DC for California, where we thought we could finally stop paying so much attention to politics. But then 2016 came along, and the rest is . . . not even close to history.

We started *Pod Save America* and Crooked Media because, like slightly more than half the electorate, we were alarmed by what Donald Trump and his coterie of goons would do to our democracy, which – let's be honest – had a few issues before they arrived on the scene. Through the pod, we met a lot of anxious people – online, during live shows, when we looked in the mirror – who felt the same way. Many had never participated in politics before. Everywhere we went, we heard the same questions: "What can I do?" "Where do I begin?" "Is Lovett always on?" (Sadly, he is!)

Democracy or Else is an effort to put down on paper the lessons we've learned along the way, lessons that will hopefully transform you into a savvier, saner, well-armed citizen (well-armed with *knowledge*!). We've also gathered advice from some of the best organizers and least annoying politicians around – people who've tangled with America's top dumbasses and wannabe tyrants and lived to tell the tale. Because, if the roller-coaster ride of doom and hope we've been on for the past few years has taught us anything, it's that no one has all the answers. We all have a role to play in figuring this shit out, and doing it together is actually the fun part.

Over the course of these ten chapters, you will develop the skills to:

- Get engaged

- Stay informed

- Vote

- Donate

- Volunteer

- Organize

- Work in politics

- Run for office

- Keep alight the tiny, twinkling spark of wonder in your soul that scientists call "hope"

So let the ~~nightmare slog~~ adventure begin!

Welcome to the most important election guide of our lifetime.

Step 1

BE PREPARED

SO YOUR COUNTRY is currently experiencing a precipitous descent into fascism and you'd like to pump the breaks on that. Great! You've chosen to act on that dull, queasy feeling that's telling you to do *something* before (preferably before!) it's too late.

The first step in the battle to save American democracy is to understand the wildly imperfect, maddeningly frustrating political system we've inherited from the founders (geniuses, all of them). Is it tempting to look out at our exquisitely shattered society and doubt that it can ever be fixed? Sure, just as it can be tempting to think there are simple, obvious solutions to our problems that the people in charge are too incompetent or craven to fight for (sometimes true!). But you picked up this book because you still believe that our politics CAN change, and that all of us – not just politicians – can play a role in changing it, even if our political system was built to make that process hard and slow. So you need to know how the system works, how it doesn't, and what it'll take to improve it. And that requires just a touch of civics . . .

Oh No, History

The United States is often called "the world's oldest democracy." (Just don't tell the Greeks! Or women or Black people or Native Americans or those Palm Beach Jews who accidentally voted for Pat Buchanan in 2000.) We've been around for 248 years and made a ton of memories. But our longevity also makes America a little bit like the first iPod: changed the game, now just a brick with sticky buttons. We ushered in the era of "government by the people" as opposed to "government by inbred Habsburg," but when it comes to liberty, age doesn't come before beauty: according to the latest Democracy Index – out of the 167 countries and territories analyzed – the United States ranked 30th. Which is honestly higher than we expected. The index evaluates countries in five key categories: functioning of government, political participation, political culture, civil liberties, and the likelihood a loser president will try to overturn an election, then grab all the secret war plans he can stuff in his pockets. The US is what the index has deemed to be a "flawed" democracy, which is just one category above "government the CIA would've tried to overthrow in the '80s."

We know what you're thinking. "Flawed? Hey Democracy Index, why don't you fuck off to Denmark?!" But once you calm down, you'll realize: it's true. The Supreme Court has overturned decades of progress thanks to some of the most extreme justices to ever get a lifetime appointment. An insurrectionist took a shit on Nancy Pelosi's desk, which is *not* allowed on the tour. One of America's two major political parties has radicalized in pretty dangerous and stupid ways. And these doofs have succeeded in part by preying on cynicism and on frustration with the way our system works – even when it's working as designed.

More than anything, America's founders wanted to ~~kill witches~~ prevent this new country from backsliding into monarchy, which is why they created a structure that would make it very difficult for a game show host with tyrannical tendencies to roast-joke his way into a quasi-dictatorship.

The founders understood that power corrupts so, in America, power is divided – between our three equal branches of government, between the federal government and the states, blah blah blah. But these safeguards weren't just about limiting the power of leaders at the top – the founders were afraid of the people at the bottom too. It's why, when the Constitution was ratified, only white men with property were allowed to vote. It's also why senators weren't elected directly by voters until the passage of the 17th Amendment. Or why we don't get to vote for president, but for an "Electoral College" instead.

Were the founders right to worry that voters might be too easily swayed by a demagogue? Yeah, turn on the news. But the founders were also toothless slave owners and lead-poisoned shopkeepers. They railed against the dangers of political parties, but they didn't put enough (or anything) in the Constitution to protect against the danger those parties might pose. Dividing power between different branches and levels of government doesn't do much good if a major party is unified and radicalized against government itself.

Our challenge is to save a democracy that's hard to change by design – even when it's under threat. After all, the struggle to fulfill the promise of equal rights and dignity to every American has always been more difficult than the struggle to deny that promise. It took almost 100 years to abolish slavery, 144 years for women to get the right to vote, and 239 years to legalize marriage equality (and we still don't have an Equal Rights Amendment).

But there's always a way forward. There's always a chance to wring more democracy and more progress out of a system that feels broken, even rigged. The key is to figure out what can actually be changed and how.

Fortunately, we've developed a highly scientific rating scale to help you determine just how difficult it will be to fix various parts of our political system.

THE SENATE

DIFFICULTY RATING

Why do 40 million people in California get the same number of senators as 580,000 people in Wyoming? To enrage liberals forever. And because ratifying the Constitution takes compromise with smaller states. The founders did not envision two political parties in which one party's voters would mostly live in the densely populated areas of bigger states and the other party's voters would spread across the country's sparsely populated small towns and rural areas. But that's what happened.

"So let's be legends and give California more senators!" We love the energy, but sadly, the Constitution is explicit: every state gets an equal vote in the Senate, and no amendment can change that unless ALL states agree, and they won't because Idaho and Vermont would tell Texas and New York to eat shit. One thing we can and should do is make DC and Puerto Rico states – because the Americans who live there are NOT second class citizens and DESERVE equal representation. And sure, they'd probably vote for Democratic senators but that wasn't even a factor in our rationale and shame on you for thinking so little of us. But statehood requires overcoming or eliminating the filibuster (more on that later), and it still doesn't fully solve the Senate's small-state bias. And so, there are only three other options: (1) convince 200,000 liberals who are sick of paying $4,000 in rent for a one-bedroom apartment in San Francisco to move to Anchorage, (2) split California in half (no bad ideas in a brainstorm!), and/or (3) WIN ELECTIONS. That's it.

THE CONSTITUTION

DIFFICULTY RATING

Just proposing an amendment to the Constitution requires approval from two-thirds of Congress or a convention proposed by two-thirds of the states, and then ratification requires approval from three-quarters of all states. It's nearly impossible to convince just over half of Congress to keep the government open. And given how hard people fight over parking spots these days, the constitutional convention route seems a bit fraught. But hey, the most recent amendment to the Constitution wasn't added all that long ago. In 1982, a sophomore at the University of Texas named Gregory Watson wrote a paper about a long-forgotten amendment originally drafted by James Madison in 1789 that would prevent members of Congress from raising their own salaries without first facing re-election. The amendment never went anywhere, and the paper got a C, but thanks to Greg, it was finally ratified a decade later. Reach for the stars!

THE ELECTORAL COLLEGE (AMERICA'S WORST SAFETY SCHOOL)

DIFFICULTY RATING

Instead of a national popular vote, the presidency is a state-by-state contest where (except for in Maine and Nebraska), the candidate who wins the popular vote in each state gets all of that state's electoral votes – which equal the state's number of House members plus two senators. Whoever wins more than half the electoral votes (270) wins the presidency, unless the ghost of Hugo Chávez futzes with the voting machines again. It's all very stupid. But why does the Electoral College exist in the first place? And hey, is it because of slavery? Pretty much, yeah. A national popular vote (which was proposed!) would have disadvantaged southern states because enslaved people couldn't cast ballots. But an electoral vote based on each state's congressional delegation leveled the playing field for southern slave-owning states. And it's worked out great except for the five times it's gone horribly wrong.

One way to change this is by changing the Constitution (we see the pattern here). Another possible solution is the "National Popular Vote Interstate Compact," in which states agree to award their electoral votes to whichever candidate wins the national popular vote. But that requires states totaling 270 electoral votes to agree (so far we're at 205), and also for the Supreme Court to decide that it's constitutional. Which brings us to . . .

THE SUPREME COURT

DIFFICULTY RATING

Not a fan of ultraconservative justices ruling against basic human rights? Well, they get to keep their jobs until the gavel is pried from their cold, dead hands, they get impeached, or they choose to retire. (Go for it, Clarence! Life begins at 70. Gas up the RV!) If that doesn't sound like the best way to run a rodeo, Congress can pass laws to change the number of justices who sit on the court and/or how long they serve. And that wouldn't be the first time it did. The number of justices changed six times before we landed on the current total of nine in 1869. Changing it again would require 60 votes in the Senate to break a filibuster (it's coming, we promise).

GERRYMANDERING

DIFFICULTY RATING

The practice where politicians get to pick their own voters by drawing maps with the most politically favorable congressional and state legislative districts. It's like if you were running for your neighborhood council but were able to exclude the homes where your dog shits on the front lawn every morning. Gerrymandering can be changed by state laws (which can be tough to pass, especially if the state legislature is . . . gerrymandered) or by a national law, but again, that requires 60 votes in the Senate. And about that . . .

THE FILIBUSTER

DIFFICULTY RATING

Senators used to be able to debate any bill or nomination for as long as they wanted. By 1917, they decided that was dumb, so the Senate created a rule that said if 67 senators (later changed to 60) agree to end the interminably long debate (what they called "filibustering"), they'd be forced to stop and vote. But because the Senate has always been chockablock with top-notch assholes, over the next half century, the filibuster wound up being used over and over again by southern senators (see: Strom Thurmond) to block civil rights legislation. So even if there was a Senate majority in favor of a civil rights bill, there weren't 67 votes to end the debate and force a vote.

Now, what was once the exception has become the rule: most legislation requires 60 votes to overcome a potential filibuster. And since neither party has had 60 votes in the Senate in more than a decade, it means a lot of really important stuff can't get done. The good news is the party with a majority in the Senate can eliminate the filibuster with just 51 votes, and Democrats were just two votes away from getting rid of it when they tried to pass voting rights legislation in 2022. Which means what we really have to change is . . .

POLITICIANS

DIFFICULTY RATING

This you can do! We have elections every year all across the country at all different levels of government. Does gerrymandering and voter suppression make winning those elections tougher? Of course. Does too much money in politics drown out other voices? For sure. But to change any of this, we'll need to elect better people within the system we currently have. And that will require changing the minds of fellow citizens who may not want to vote for our candidate or may not want to vote at all. It will also require us to let go of the stuff we can't do anything about – like how few people live in South Dakota.

TACO BELL PUTTING THE CHEESE ON TOP OF THE LETTUCE, INSTEAD OF ON THE MEAT, SO IT DOESN'T MELT

DIFFICULTY RATING

Changing how a multinational restaurant conglomerate with more than 7,000 locations assembles its signature meat delivery system is no easy feat. But who likes it this way? The cheese all falls out. It makes no sense. And fixing it costs literally nothing. The cheese bucket just needs to slide over like two spaces. And if we could convince Taco Bell to make this change, then you know what? Del Taco could be next. Maybe one day, Miss Chipotle herself. And if that happened, would it be a tiny inspirational story about how, even if it's silly and small, we can still make a difference? If we can't do this, can we do anything? And if we can do this, what can't we do?

·

———

Alexandria Ocasio-Cortez

On change

America has always been a story of people who want, of some folks who want to cling to their own small vestiges of power and prevent us from progressing, and those who have been able to galvanize and bring us together and move us forward. And it's always a stutter step between those two things in that move towards progress.

There's no getting around the need to *persuade* people who don't think like us and whose Netflix algorithm would shake us to our very cores. But on the bright side, it could be worse. And it has been worse, here and elsewhere. Before you get too down on democracy, it's worth remembering what Winston Churchill once said while having a soak in the tub: "Democracy is the worst form of government except for all those other forms that have been tried . . . Ignore those bubbles."

Ben Rhodes

Former Deputy National Security Advisor and speechwriter for President Obama, co-host of *Pod Save the World*, and author of *New York Times* bestsellers *The World As It Is* and *After the Fall: The Rise of Authoritarianism in the World We've Made*

What makes American democracy exceptional?

When you look comparatively at different systems, you start to realize that there's no such thing as the "right" democracy. That said, I think where American democracy excels goes back to the Bill of Rights. We are a more diverse country than just about any other country on Earth. We do have a value of freedom of expression and freedom of assembly that is not perfect, but that is, more often than not, much more robust than just about any other country on Earth. It's interesting, our society is usually ahead of our government on a lot of things. Civil rights movements are way ahead of where the government is. The space for movements to emerge in America has been larger than in other countries. And movements have accomplished more in this country than they have in most other democracies. It's never been the case that we could simply count on the fact of our constitution, or our system of government, because our constitution and government tolerated slavery for almost a century, tolerated Jim Crow for almost a century, tolerated the Chinese Exclusion Act, tolerated women not having the right to vote. So there's nothing inherent in what our founding fathers did that makes us exceptional. It's the lived reality of how you practice democracy.

Just look at what we left behind:

MONARCHY VS. DEMOCRACY

WHO'S IN CHARGE

KING

YOU

WHY?

MYTH OF DIVINE SELECTION
LENS LEGITIMACY TO
INBRED WARLORDS.

INALIENABLE RIGHTS,
BITCH

HOW MONARCHIES FAIL

WITHOUT DEMOCRATIC ACCOUNTABILITY, THINGS
GET PRETTY HEADSY-HEADSY SLICEY-SLICEY

And a few other political formulas . . .

DICTATORSHIP = MONARCHY – PIZZAZZ

THEOCRACY = DICTATORSHIP + MAGIC

OLIGARCHY = DICTATORSHIP + STOCKS!

ANARCHY = FREEDOM – RESPONSIBILITY

TECHNO-UTOPIAN ISLAND NATION
NOT YET RECOGNIZED BY THE UN =
LIBERTARIANISM – WOMEN

You Never Forget Your First Job

My first job in politics was interning for Senator Ted Kennedy in the summer of 2002. Kennedy had a lot of faults (no need to tweet "Chappaquiddick" at me!) but he also dedicated his life to fighting for unions, universal health care, and civil rights, and did a lot of good. 2002 was a weird year to move to Washington. The country was gripped with fear after 9/11. Someone had sent letters laced with anthrax to news outlets and the US Senate.

The so-called "DC sniper" was shooting at random people in DC, Maryland, and Virginia. My tasks were menial: delivering mail (the paper kind!), answering phones, filing things? (It was a long time ago, I don't totally remember.) Was my internship in Kennedy's office glamorous? No. Was it paid? Also no. Did it help me get a job on Capitol Hill? Again, no, and I'd appreciate it if you'd stop peppering me with questions. But that summer got me hooked on politics. It was my gateway drug. I saw up close how the Bush administration was jamming through terrible policies and steamrolling Democrats in Congress who were supposed to be the opposition, and I knew that I wanted to help the people who were willing to fight back.

 In 2002, I interned in Senator John Kerry's press office (right down the hall from Tommy, though we never met...Or did we?). I got a lot of coffees and lunches, answered a lot of phones, and once had to transfer an entire Rolodex into a BlackBerry. (Neither of those things exist now.) I eventually got to do a little writing, and one night, Kerry's communications director asked if I'd be interested in drafting an op-ed they wanted to place in the *Boston Herald* from the senator about Martin Luther King Day. I leapt at the offer, stayed up until 3 am writing, and emailed my draft. The next day, I heard nothing back. A few days later, I checked the *Herald* and saw the op-ed, which included . . . three lines from my draft. I was THRILLED. Couldn't believe how good it felt. And after a few months of spending every day

listening to the senator's press and political teams talk about the presidential campaign they'd soon launch, I decided that when I graduated college in spring of 2003, I would do whatever I could to join them.

 I will never forget the day it became clear how much of a difference I could make in politics. All I wanted was for Jodie Foster to notice me. To care about me. To see how much I loved her. And I realized there was a perfect way to get her attention: shooting President Ronald Reagan.

———

Recent polls show a majority of Americans have lost faith in our democratic system. Confidence in our institutions has plummeted. According to a 2023 Gallup poll, 27 percent of Americans have a lot of faith in the Supreme Court, 26 percent have a lot of faith in the presidency, and for Congress that number goes all the way down to 8 percent. There is creeping cynicism everywhere you look. And in turn that cynicism becomes a weapon for politicians and interests who want nothing more than for people – especially young people – to give up and turn away from politics. Our job is to break that vicious cycle. To show, not just tell, how much good we can really do. And to prove that while it may be mind-numbingly exhausting, the work of democracy is worth it.

Still with us? Hey, nobody said this was gonna be easy. Well, OK, we did . . . but that's the thing about politics: lying is part of it.

And congrats, by the way. We just survived the most annoying part of this book to read or write. Civics complete.

What Have We Learned?

- Only you can prevent Reichstag fires
- Taco Bell should put the cheese directly on the meat so it melts
- Headsy-headsy slicey-slicey

Step 2

GET INFORMED

SO YOU'RE IN on saving democracy, and you've got a sense of the challenges ahead. One of them is knowing what the hell you're talking about. That's right: it's time to turn on the news. But what kind of news and on which screen? In today's fractured media environment, there's a seemingly endless stream of information and opinion, so it's harder than ever to figure out what's real, what's exaggerated, and what's an unhinged conspiracy that gets you an "lol so true" from Elon Musk.

You know how they say history is written by the winners? Well, the present is written by losers. OK, OK, that's not fair. The present is also narrated by investigative reporters, civic-minded writers and policy experts, hot TV anchors who still try (sup, Jake Tapper), and countless others who devote their lives to the hard and often thankless work of telling us what's actually going on in the world. But they are not alone! They are joined in this marketplace of ideas by anti-woke former *SNL* cast members, crypto dead-enders, and Kennedy heirs who did their own research.

You'll often hear people harken back to the good old days when the news seemed less noisy. They'll mention someone named Wilbur Cromkite (sic?) and how before MSNBC and Fox News, there was no such thing as "liberal" or "conservative" facts. We all used to gather round the fireplace and watch a 30-minute nonpartisan news program while collectively agreeing on what happened over the previous 24 hours. Beatles: here. Men: moon. Nixon: toast.

There is some truth to this: nonpartisan journalism – from local newspapers to national magazines to television broadcasts – reached more people and held more sway. That, in turn, shaped our political climate. Nixon really was toast, after all. It's hard to imagine, but once the president's malfeasance became public and undeniable (via the best kind of journalism – the kind that later becomes a movie), he had to resign, or he'd be removed from office. The Watergate hearings and dogged reporting took Nixon's approval rating from 67 percent at the beginning of his second term to 24 percent by the time he resigned. Simpler times . . .

Still, this golden age wasn't all golden. If a small group of people who mostly look the same are telling the same story, then a lot of other people aren't being heard. That conformity came at a price, and whether through the underground press of the 1960s, the AIDS movement of the 1980s, or right-wing media in the 1990s (three equally awesome groups), a growing number of people with diverse views and backgrounds saw the proliferation of new outlets and platforms as an opportunity to grab the megaphone. And though this cultural shift began decades ago, social media really tied up the loose ends, like Michael Corleone at the end of *The Godfather*.

The Misinformation-Industrial Complex

The internet has made it easier and cheaper to compete with legacy news outlets for attention. The result? An existential crisis for journalism: Local news and smaller outlets have been decimated as ad revenue has shifted to larger outlets and platforms like Facebook and Google. Network and cable news are hemorrhaging viewers. Even digital media companies are collapsing as the competition for eyeballs and ad dollars grows ever more intense. Everyone feels overwhelmed by this onslaught. Misinformation is like Panera Bread: terrible and everywhere. So, how do you maintain a healthy media diet when the buffet is endless and half the chafing dishes are filled with bullshit? Great question. Let's grab a plate.

Social Media

About half of US adults get at least some of their news from social media. And that makes sense. There's a little something for everyone. Hoping to see a sitting member of Congress double down on Holocaust denial or a college professor explain why there can be no ethical consumption of oat milk under capitalism? Hello, Twitter (or whatever it's called now). Are you a teen just forming your own identity and searching for an endless torrent of perfect bodies and curated existences until you can't look at yourself in the mirror with any emotion other than shame? Check out Instagram. Curious how many catalytic converters have been stolen within a two-block radius of your house? Download the Nextdoor app. Want to watch a drunk pharmaceutical rep get kicked off her flight to Phoenix? You're going to love TikTok. Yes, social media can raise your blood pressure while totally warping your sense of yourself and the real world, but that's what makes it so fun.

Pros
- Big news tends to break here first
- Experts explaining complicated stuff for likes
- Make friends for life you never have to meet in person
- Feel-good videos of gorillas delighted by magic tricks and kids coming out of anesthesia
- An avenue for discovering funny, smart, weird people who never had a platform before

Cons

- Sucks you in like a whirlpool of human shit

- Dummies explaining why the experts are wrong

- The algorithm that determines what you see is programmed by an alt-right billionaire

- Can lead to a sudden, uncontrollable urge to join the discourse without knowing all (or any) of the facts

- An avenue for discovering the most confident and awful people who never had a platform before

⚡ DON'T FEED THE TROLLS! ⚡

LOOK OUT! YOU ARE ENTERING SOCIAL MEDIA. THIS IS A WILDERNESS AREA. REMEMBER: YOU ARE BUT A VISITOR. DO NOT DISTURB THE WILDLIFE. THIS IS THEIR HOME.

BEEF CON:

Right-wing influencer, believes that men are meant to eat meat and only meat and that women are meant to be subservient. Claims to have unlocked the secret to happiness, is on steroids, and currently somehow getting divorced twice at the same time.

THE CONTRARIAN:

The only sane and smart person, believes there are extremists on both sides, in the sense that arsonists and firefighters are both around a lot of fire. Is just asking questions, but those questions always seem to involve why you can't say anything anymore without being canceled, even though they say every goddamn thing that comes to mind.

BROKEN WINE MOM:

This poor good soul. She does everything. She donates to everyone. When she can't sleep she imagines what it would be like to watch *Suits* with Rachel Maddow. But seeing her neighbors in suburban Ohio vote for Trump broke her spirit, and she hasn't let her phone screen lock since November 8, 2016.

Kara Swisher

Award-winning journalist with decades of experience covering the tech industry, currently serves as contributing editor of *New York* magazine, host of the podcasts *On with Kara Swisher* and *Pivot*.

The dangers of doomscrolling

You need to stop doing it. It's bad for your health, it's bad for your mentality. And a lot of it is not factual. You know, a lot of people always ask me, "What am I scared of?" I'm scared of scary things, not everything. And I don't get angry about everything. And so what you should do is find the trusted news sources. You can find that anywhere. You can find it on Twitter, you find it on Threads, you can find it in individual Substacks. I have a very varied diet, but I still do stick to the news organizations I trust, such as the *New York Times* or the *Washington Post* or the *Wall Street Journal*. And you should also, lastly, think of different points of view. Different points of view are critical for you to understand how people are feeling. It doesn't mean you have to agree with them.

If you don't like what's happening with tribalism on the right wing – and it's happening very clearly – don't do it on the left wing. Just don't do it. The whole point of being a liberal is to be open-minded. Not necessarily to accept everything everyone says, but at least you don't have to scream at every moment of the day.

And here's the thing. There are people out there every day, fighting the good fight on social media. Arguing, dunking, stitching, and quote tweeting, and God bless 'em. But before you dunk on a dumb post, or get in an argument with a stranger, or duet a video to tell us why the person who thinks they're the hero of a first date is actually the villain, remember: social media is not real life (and if it is your real life, get a better one).

☆ AS HEARD ON <u>POD SAVE AMERICA</u> ☆

Rachel Maddow

On our changing media habits

We really do have people cutting the cord. People not having access. People not watching television. People not accessing traditional print media in the same way that they used to. And people being more online, purely online, in terms of their information gathering. The resulting media landscape is less live news and less remunerative live news and more fractured in terms of the right-wing stuff getting really kooky. And so I don't know what that's gonna do in the long run. I don't think people have less appetite for information. But there's gonna be less traditionally curated and edited live daily news sources that are consumed by people under the age of 50 for the foreseeable future.

Cable News

Ah, cable news. Once upon a time, Jon Stewart went on a nightly screaming match called *Crossfire* and said, "Stop hurting America." (It was a whole thing!) Of course, Stewart wasn't arguing that all cable news coverage was bad. Cable news has lots of great reporters, but since its inception, the fear has always been that cable news would turn us into a bunch of anxious, addled info freaks with no attention spans. (And here we are.) Cable news got millions hooked on horse race coverage and the never-ending news cycle. But younger viewers are "cutting the cord," and older viewers are "slipping the surly bonds of earth." And that's two ways to leave a lover, you know?

What will become of CNN, MSNBC, and the channel that makes retired contractors in Tampa so angry that they fire shotguns through their front doors when the bell rings? Who knows! The future, like that apology note to your coworker for barfing on her sweater during last year's holiday party, is unwritten.

Pros

- Everything you could ever hope to know about every Category 3 Storm for as long as you live

- Has transformed election night coverage into an Electoral College bowl game. It's annoying, but we honestly love it

- Lively talking heads who can make the same information sound different IF THEY YELL IT

Cons

- Programming that panders to the politics of the audience (which we hate!)

- Overhyped chyrons like "BREAKING NEWS: Titanic Sunk 102 Years Ago Tonight," which was real

- Every major cable news outlet has at one point employed Tucker Carlson
- Why we all know the phrase "moderate to severe plaque psoriasis"

Print

According to a 2023 report from the Medill School of Journalism at Northwestern, almost a third of our nation's newspapers have shut down since 2005, and we are losing an average of two more papers every week. In fact, there's a chance that print media will be dead by the time you read this. And that's a shame because newspapers have been helping Americans get the fireplace going since the 1700s. This is the medium that broke Watergate and the Boston Catholic Church abuse scandal. Without the *New York Times*, we wouldn't have read the Pentagon Papers or learned what kind of house you can get for $800,000 in three different cities. And without the *New York Post*, we wouldn't have colorful headlines like "Weiner Exposed" or "Weiner's Second Coming!" or "Weiner Roast" or "Hide the Weiner." All good. But now, print is going digital. The *New York Times* is where you play Candy Crush for smart people.

Pros
- Long-form, in-depth coverage
- The finest investigative reporting from all over the world
- Tends to have the highest journalistic standards around (unless owned by a Murdoch)

Cons

- On the pricey side – gotta pay up for those subscriptions
- They can get a little carried away with the desire to service very fine readers on both sides
- Massively overestimate the demand for sudoku

Podcasts

The perfect medium, the perfect art. Radio but on your phone, newspapers but in your ear, friends but on the toilet. A 2023 survey found that 42 percent of Americans age 12 or older had listened to a podcast in the last month. You can find podcasts about anything – true crime, sports, news, politics – but it's important that you do some light investigation into the hosts (you have our bios) so that you're not just getting misinformation in between ads for Liver King supplements.

Pros

- Listen to your favorite former Obama staffers deliver promo codes for underwear with pizzazz
- Length is not a problem (wink), so hosts can go deeper (wink) on complicated topics (no wink)
- Many great independent options outside of the traditional mainstream media

Cons

- Ted Cruz has one
- Little to no editorial oversight
- Proliferation of Obama bros

Local News

The go-to place for live coverage of any animal that escapes from the zoo. Americans tend to trust local news more than national news, but they probably shouldn't. For example, a lot of local television news stations were acquired by the conservative Sinclair Broadcast Group, whose programming reaches tens of millions of American households. And they've really made the most of it – forcing affiliates to air "must-run" segments designed to keep area grandmas focused on the real threat: an ISIS caravan invading us from Mexico.

But right-wing media isn't the only problem impacting local newspapers, radio, and TV stations. Changing business models have left countless local news outlets understaffed if they've been able to keep their lights on at all. And that's a tragedy. Local reporters are often the last line of defense against old-school local corruption, where a sketchy alderman pockets an envelope full of cash and suddenly they're fracking under the hospital. Local reporters take on skeezy landlords, city council members with expensive taste and – equally important – they help us find out why a car drove into that 7-Eleven. (Medical emergency? Robbery? Drugs? You can't tell from the sidewalk. That takes REPORTING. What we're saying is, one of the simplest and most effective ways you can support local journalism is by driving your car into a 7-Eleven.)

Pros
- Human interest stories about what's going on in your community
- Hey, look – your son's debate team is on TV!
- The best bloopers in the biz

Cons

- Can sometimes be a right-wing outlet in disguise
- Slightly overestimates the demand for high-speed-car-chase content
- Makes you think the only things that happen in your city are high school football games and grisly murders

Last and least informatively . . .

Right-Wing Media

Hey, ever wonder why more than two out of three Republicans believe Joe Biden lost the 2020 election? Or why there are so many videos of middle-aged women screaming at the assistant manager of a Target because of a shirt that says, "Gay for Summer"? Turns out, pumping out nonstop misinformation and rage for decades really messes with people's brains. That's why one of the biggest threats to journalism (and democracy) is the rise of Fox News, right-wing radio, and the proliferation of propaganda outlets like Newsmax, InfoWars, Breitbart, podcasts hosted by mixed martial artists, and other creatures of the manosphere. It's a well-oiled machine that keeps the audience jacked up on conspiracy theories, manufactured scandals, and dietary supplements, for some reason. "Democrats are evil. Cities are hellscapes. Jesus was a venture capitalist." It's also highly lucrative because the right is especially good at preying on the fears of their audience. And it's easier to get old people to spend their retirement savings on gold coins once you've convinced them that the global economy is about to collapse.

Pros

- Great for anyone who feels the mainstream media doesn't devote enough air time to the over-sexualization of Ninja Turtles
- Politicians who cater to right-wing media end up sounding like culture war freaks, and alienate the mainstream voters who worry more about "where to get insulin" than "where we pee"
- Anti-Disney tirades could reduce wait times for the Star Wars rides

Cons

- Turns every single policy disagreement into a matter of personal identity
- Went anti-vax even though the vaccine could have been Trump's biggest accomplishment!
- It's way too simple to say "everything is fucked up because of right-wing media," but is it?

☆ AS HEARD ON POD SAVE AMERICA ☆

Jon Stewart

On right-wing media

For 60 years, if you have an AM radio, 24 hours a day, they preach Democrats as enemies. In no uncertain terms. They are raising a generation to feel as though those people are enemies. And it blows my mind that they play victim to this day. But what they do so effectively is they provide the infrastructure for that propaganda. And they do it really, really well.

Dan Pfeiffer

Beloved co-host of *Pod Save America*, sex symbol, former Senior Advisor and White House Communications Director to President Obama, author of *New York Times* bestsellers including *Un-Trumping America* and *Battling the Big Lie: How Fox, Facebook, and the MAGA Media Are Destroying America*.

Why isn't progressive media as influential as right-wing media?

Fox has outsized influence for a couple of reasons. One, they have a much bigger presence on social, particularly Facebook, and so those clips are being shared and being pumped by the Facebook algorithm to a lot of people. The other thing is that Fox is also, in large parts of the country, sort of background noise in all places you go. If you go to Jiffy Lube in rural America and you're waiting in the waiting room, Fox is on. They would never put CNN on.

Democratic politicians, for the most part, feel a little dirty about progressive media. Like it's not real. Like they should really be on *Meet the Press* and CNN. That's real media. If I'm on *Pod Save America* or the *Young Turks* or something else, that's not real press. What we need more Democrats to realize, particularly in this media age, is that the only way to communicate directly with our voters is through progressive media. Progressive organizations should be advertising on progressive media. They should be doing interviews with progressive media. They should be giving news to progressive media.

Mind Over Media

Research has shown that our obsession with breaking news is breaking us. In 2017, a majority of Americans said that regularly following current events stressed them out. And that was *before* the pandemic made us all so chill. Think back to the first, second, third, and fourth time (as of this writing) you heard that Donald Trump was indicted. Or when you got a push notification that Kanye declared "death con 3" on the Jews. The news can rev you up or leave you down in the dumps. And that's fine. You just have to make sure that consuming the news doesn't consume you.

We live in an attention economy. Your attention is the commodity that everyone (including us) is after. (And if you're still reading this, we did it! We're inside your head.) Please, show your attention the care it needs. Your attention is an orchid, sensitive to heat and light and videos where a person born after 9/11 explains why skinny jeans are the new dad jeans. We're all human. Few of us are truly strong enough to resist our personalized, custom dopamine drip of 21st century content. Maybe your guilty pleasure is binging on Democratic Twitter and topping it off with an hour on your burner Truth Social account, or watching TikToks of road rage dashcams. Give yourself a cheat day – spend the afternoon doomscrolling on the couch in your soft pants. Everything is OK in moderation. Ultimately, you have to find the media diet that works for you. But here's a few things to keep in mind as you do . . .

TIPS FOR A HEALTHY MEDIA DIET

- Have some basic standards! Rely on outlets that employ actual journalists and/or people with real political experience, have editors and fact-checkers, issue corrections, and don't get sued for billions of dollars because they promoted election conspiracy theories.

- Read or watch the entire piece. Don't settle for the headline, the screenshot, or the cable news chyron. They can't bury the lede if you're willing to dig deep enough. And most issues are way too complex to be understood via Instagram carousel. If a conflict has remained unresolved for thousands of years, for example, a 30-second video probably won't get to the bottom of it.

- Don't take the clickbait! Before reposting a story, find out if at least one other news outlet has reported it, especially if it relies mostly on anonymous and/or background sources.

- Try keeping up with the Alex Joneses. Challenge yourself to seek out opinions and analysis that don't just confirm your beliefs and biases. Don't be afraid to peek in on Steve Bannon's *War Room* podcast, a MAGA fever dream that Tommy listens to with concerning frequency so that he can hear about the most deranged conspiracies before they spread to Fox News and Donald Trump's second inaugural.

- Figure out which influencers you can really trust (the hot ones) and which podcasts you can really trust (only ours).

- The surgeon general recommends that you DO NOT follow every poll, but if you have to, please poll responsibly. Which means understanding that polls are just a snapshot in time, that they are sometimes wrong or off by a couple of points, and that they are far more useful when averaged.

- Embrace nontraditional media. It's not going anywhere, so we must harness its power for good. There are really smart people making deeply researched shows on YouTube. There are thoughtful debates happening while people play *Zelda* on Twitch.

- Feel free to criticize the media when they make mistakes (we've made a living off of it!), but keep in mind that the media isn't a cause, it's a business. Don't expect Maggie Haberman to save democracy. That's *your* job.

And in case you're not sure what a sample media meal plan looks like . . .

FAVREAU'S MEDIA PLAN

Breakfast, 5 am

- Listen to a news or politics podcast on my walk to Starbucks.

- Read Playbook, Punchbowl News, Axios, the Message Box, and other assorted newsletters in my inbox.

- Read top stories in the *New York Times*, the *Washington Post*, and *Politico*.

- Read stories posted in the Crooked Media Slack channel or sent on various text chains.

- Get distracted from all of this by texts, Slacks, WhatsApps, Twitter, and ultimately my toddler.

Snack, 10 am

- Read stories posted in Crooked Media's Slack, engage in lighthearted banter, make a few jokes!

- Scroll through Twitter, become distracted by the day's petty outrage, bookmark a few stories that I will not read later.

Lunch, 12 pm

- Read the first few paragraphs of that *Atlantic/New Yorker* piece people keep recommending. Oh no, it's 5,000 words?

- Open Twitter, scroll, click, back to work.

Snack, 4 pm

- Two more paragraphs of the *Atlantic/New Yorker* piece. Why do they make them so long now?

- Did I miss any tweets? Nope, got 'em all.

Dinner, 6 pm

- Read nightly newsletters, open tabs, latest headlines, and the next few paragraphs of that *Atlantic/New Yorker* piece that . . . seems to be getting even longer?

Bedtime, 10 pm

- Listen to a pod or read a book as a way to distract from grappling with existential angst.

- Tell myself that tomorrow, I'll finish that *Atlantic/New Yorker* piece.

———

And that's the news. Now you have to make it news you can use, which we'll cover in our next chapter.

Good night, and good luck.

What Have We Learned?

- Social media is not real life
- We are the only podcasters you can trust
- Wilbur Cromkite

Step 3

VOTE EARLY AND OFTEN

WE'VE NOW REACHED the getting-off-your-couch portion of the journey. You've got some credible(ish) info coursing through your veins and you're ready to go out there and take action. So where do you start? By voting. It's literally the least you can do. And yet, many Americans don't. The 2020 election saw the highest turnout rate in 120 years, and it was still just under 67 percent of eligible voters. We were on the verge of spending a second term with a serial abuser of women (and power), and a third of the country stayed home! Now you may be thinking, "Hey, I voted! Why are you guys telling me all this?" Well, why are you being so fucking defensive?!

Voting can't fix everything, but without voting, we can't fix anything. The only way we pass new laws is by electing people who fight to bring about the change we want to see. The only way to clean up our mess of a political system is to get our hands in the muck. As hockey great Wayne Gretzky famously said, "You miss 100% of the shots you don't take." Well, elections are a lot like hockey – constant fighting, the Canadians are better at it than us, and there are a surprising number of Russians involved. The point is, whether your party nominates the most charismatic politician on the planet or a 2,000-year-old man, you have to vote. It's not about them. It's about you. It's about which of the candidates is most likely to use their office to improve your life and your community.

We may be preaching to the choir on this (and don't have perfect voting records ourselves, so we're not trying to scold anyone . . . yet), but even if you're a regular voter, you have an important role to play in getting the people around you to be regular voters too. Some of that work is about removing barriers that make it harder to vote, some of it is persuading people who don't always think voting is worthwhile, and we can't just wait until a few months before an election to get started. As we like to say, there are no off years.

There Are No Off Years

The way things have been going, every election could be our last. Or at least that should be your mentality. In 2020, the final outcome came down to about 43,000 votes in three states. 43,000! Joe Biden got 81 million votes – more than any presidential candidate ever. And yet, out of more than 155 million votes cast, his total margin in the three closest swing states – Arizona, Georgia, and Wisconsin – was slightly less than the population of Sheboygan! That's too close! And so politicians (Republicans) are spending a lot of time and money making it more difficult for certain people (who aren't Republicans) to vote. Because in a razor-thin election, a few people in a few precincts leaving a long voting line or finding out their registration was canceled can make the difference between a candidate who wants to protect abortion access and a candidate who thinks the greatest threat to democracy is a prom king in a dress.

Slow Your Voter Roll

Let's take a look at the different ways politicians can make it harder for people to vote.

Voter Suppression

In recent years, several states and counties have been pressured by the election-denier crowd to pass legislation that makes voting difficult. These measures include making it harder to vote by mail, making it easier for partisan poll watchers to intimidate voters, getting rid of Sunday early voting, refusing to let people hand out food and water to those waiting in line at the polls for extended periods of time, curtailing efforts to help voters get registered, bogus ID requirements based on lies about voter fraud, cutting the number of polling places or drop boxes, disenfranchising voters with felony convictions, and a host of other measures aimed at disproportionately hurting Democratic voters (especially Black, brown, and young Democratic voters).

Stacey Abrams

On Georgia

We are ground zero for voter suppression and proof that you can push back and push through. What we were able to do in 2020 and 2021 is a direct result of the efforts that were made in 2018 and 2019. And so we know that there is a way to navigate and circumvent and to overwhelm voter suppression. But that doesn't diminish the illegitimacy of its existence. And what is so maddening to me is this idea that just because you can fight it, that means you shouldn't have to worry about it. No, we shouldn't have to fight this hard.

The Purge

Not to be confused with the popular film franchise that makes no sense, this is a different kind of horror movie in which millions of Americans get kicked off voter rolls. Maybe the best/worst example is what happened in the state of Georgia ahead of the 2018 gubernatorial race. More than half a million voters were purged from the rolls – and those who got purged were found to be far more likely to come from . . . wait for it . . . Democratic precincts. On top of that, the Republican secretary of state who oversaw the purges, Brian Kemp, was also running for governor! In 2021, Georgia canceled another

101,000 inactive registrations. Last year, they purged almost 190,000 people from the registered voters list.

Georgia, by the way, isn't even in the top five toughest states to cast your ballot. According to the 2022 "Cost of Voting Index," the worst places to vote are New Hampshire, Mississippi, and any state where the governor is a Huckabee. Republicans have realized that winning elections with an unpopular agenda in a diversifying society requires either (a) moderating and becoming more broadly appealing to bring in new voters or (b) going full asshole in every conceivable way. Guess what they chose! But the effort to disenfranchise young and diverse voters (while cattle prodding white baby boomers with stories of ethnic Santas and woke Disney princesses) is only one of several factors preventing voter turnout from rising. Here are a few more.

Election Day Is Not a Holiday

A recent survey from the Census Bureau shows the most common reason registered voters said they didn't turn out in 2022 is that they were either too busy or had a conflicting work or school schedule. Not only is Election Day not a federal holiday – it's on a Tuesday! Has anyone ever been excited to do anything on a Tuesday? The timing of our general elections was established by Congress in 1845, when Tuesdays in November were considered to be an ideal date for farmers to go to the polls. And that would be totally fine if most Americans today headed off to the polls after feeding the chickens and tending Aunt Cora's wound before it sours. But that's not the world we're living in.

Distrust in Our Elections

According to a 2023 Pew Research poll, only 4 percent of Americans think "our political system is working extremely or very well." Who would have guessed that a bunch of right-wing politicians and pundits telling voters they shouldn't have faith in our elections would lead to a lack of faith in our elections? But for all the Big Lie super-spreaders popping off about rampant voter fraud, there have been countless investigations that prove otherwise. The Associated Press found that in the last presidential election – out of more than 25.5 million ballots cast in the six key battleground states – there were fewer than 475 possible cases of voter fraud. That means the odds of voter fraud are less than 0.0019 percent. Which is – to use some statistical jargon – pretty un-fucking-likely! You are actually three times more likely to get struck by lightning, according to the Brennan Center (a pro-democracy, anti-electrocution think tank).

While voting isn't as easy as it should be, it used to be a lot harder – in fact it used to be impossible for basically everyone. That's right, we're doing history again.

I'll Have What He's Having

When George Washington became president with 69 electoral votes (nice), only white males were allowed to vote. It wasn't until 1869 that Congress passed the 15th Amendment, which gave Black men the right to vote. Then it was another 50 years until the 19th Amendment codified women's suffrage. And in the century between the end of the Civil War and the passage of the Voting Rights Act of 1965, southern states used poll taxes where you had to pay a fee to vote, impossible literacy tests, all-white primaries, and state-sanctioned violence and terror to keep Black people from voting. Fast-forward to 2013, when the Supreme Court's conservative majority gutted the Voting Rights Act. It was quite the ruling. Their logic was basically, "Great news, everyone! Racism is over!" Or as Justice Ruth Bader Ginsburg said in her dissent, "Throwing out [a key enforcement provision of the Voting Rights Act] when it has worked and is continuing to work to stop discriminatory changes is like throwing away your umbrella in a rainstorm because you are not getting wet."

Another big expansion of voting rights took place in 1971. Congress passed and 42 states ratified the 26th Amendment to the Constitution, lowering the voting age from 21 to 18 – because if young men were old enough to be drafted into war, they were old enough to vote. Some Republicans have talked about wanting the voting age to be higher (with the exception of Matt Gaetz, who doesn't want to disenfranchise his future girlfriends). It's no wonder: in the 2022 midterm, nearly two-thirds of voters under 30 voted for Democrats in House races.

LaTosha Brown

Co-founder of *Black Votes Matter*, an organization devoted to increasing voter registration and turnout in marginalized, predominantly Black communities

Why voting matters

My grandfather was born in 1905, my grandmother in 1910. He was born in the Deep South in Alabama, and most of his adult life, he was unable to vote. He had this torn card in his wallet that he would pull out. It was a poll tax receipt. I don't think I knew exactly what it was, but I knew it had value, because even the way that he would show it, it was something that was really important. My grandmother, I would go to vote with her. She would dress up to go to vote just as if we were going to Sunday service, and she would always take her good pocketbook. At the time, the voting booths used to have these curtains, and you would go in the voting booth and pull the curtain around, and then she would actually let me pull the lever down. When she let the curtain out, it was a certain way that she held her head. It was something that she had done for herself. My grandmother didn't drive. My grandfather drove her all around. As I reflect on it now, it's the most independent that I had seen her. I didn't have the words to articulate it at the time, but I saw her embrace having power and agency. It's why I think it's so important that when we're doing this work, we're not necessarily trying to convince people to believe in a system, but we're getting people to believe in themselves. That's how we're really going to ensure that democracy is saved and how we actually get the America we desire and we deserve.

Too Close to Call

Obviously, tight presidential races are nothing new. In 1960, John F. Kennedy edged (lol) Richard Nixon in the popular vote by less than 120,000 ballots – a surprisingly close result when you consider just how hot he was. But over the last few decades, our elections have gotten closer and even more consequential. Any of you TikTokers old enough to remember the year 2000? In that election, George W. Bush "won" Florida by only 537 votes (plus five more from the Supreme Court!). If Al Gore had been like 0.0001 percent more chill in one debate, we don't get stuck with eight years of W. in the White House, there's no Iraq War, and Christian Bale doesn't have to gain 40 pounds to play Dick Cheney.

How about 2016? 80,000 votes in three states go the other way – Hillary Clinton gets to replace Ruth Bader Ginsburg with RBG's 31-year-old clone, which was going to be such an amazing surprise. Without those three Trump-appointed justices, *Roe* would still be the law of the land.

Downballot Races
Have Feelings Too

It's not enough to just show up for one presidential election every four years. You have to vote like, all the time. Sometimes downballot races happen when we're also voting for the big ones. Sometimes it's on a random day. (Pop quiz, bitch.) So you really have to pay attention. It's easy to get motivated for the main event, but sometimes the smallest races can have the biggest impact.

Look at what happened in Wisconsin in 2023, where the election of a liberal justice to the state supreme court created a liberal majority, which then ruled that the Republican gerrymander was unconstitutional. That decision led to new, fair maps, that will finally level the playing field after a decade of Republican dominance.

And as a result of Michigan Democrats winning both houses of the state legislature for the first time in 40 years, they have been able to repeal the state's draconian abortion ban, reform the tax code, pass gun control laws, protect unions, and expand LGBTQ rights.

And for those of you who are parents, there's never been a more critical time to pay attention to who is up for a seat on your school board (or run for yourself). This has become the battlefield for every culture war in America. Your vote could be the only thing stopping an overzealous board of ed from shutting down your kid's high school production of *The Best Little Whorehouse in Texas*.

There have also been a slew of victories for more progressive prosecutors and ballot initiatives that range from protecting reproductive rights to gun control. In 2022, Nebraska and Nevada voted to increase the minimum wage. New Mexico became the first state to make early-childhood education a constitutional right. Since 2018, nine states have expanded Medicaid, and sixteen states have legalized recreational weed.

Whether we build housing or fix our kids' schools or pave the roads where we text and drive, local elections matter because they are the ones that most directly affect your life and your community. Do you think windmills cause cancer? Do you hate affordable housing? Are you against bike lanes? If not, then you have to show up – because a *lot* of people disagree with you. When you don't vote in local elections, you're really voting against yourself. Or like that guy who was running for a city council seat in Rainier, Washington last year and didn't cast a ballot, then lost his race by one vote – sometimes you're LITERALLY voting against yourself.

Now you may be thinking, "I'm just one person, can I really make a difference?" Not with that attitude! If you think presidential elections are close, at the local level, there are actual TIES. Imagine you forget to vote and then you find out (and this is real, it really happens) they're flipping a coin, or drawing names from sealed envelopes, or choosing Ping-Pong balls with numbers on them and the highest number wins. If only you had shown up, you would have made the difference.

Maybe you've never missed an election, or maybe you're voting for the very first time – either way, casting your ballot comes down to these three simple words:

Make a Plan

You've probably heard this before, but we're gonna remind you again: it's essential that you make a plan. Don't get cute or cocky or assume the outcome has already been decided. (We tried that one in 2016, and here we are!) Make a plan and stick to it. And lay off the edibles in the days leading up to the election so you can remember that plan (edibles are a reward for doing your tasks). Here are, to us at least, key elements of a successful pre-election routine.

1. Make sure that you are registered to vote: elections are run by individual states, every state is different, and as we said – many states are actively trying to discourage you from voting – so be sure to check the rules for where you live.

2. Know your polling place: is it a middle school gym, a rec center, or one of those cool churches with a pride flag and a female pastor who reads lesbian from a hundred feet away?

3. Decide how you will vote: early, same day, by mail, a late-night ballot dump, there are so many options.

4. Finally, and this is a must: Drag your friends along. Make a day of it. (You may have to anyway, depending on the wait times in your state.)

The Vote-by-Mail-Dominated World

According to the Census Bureau – in the last midterm, about a third of all voters cast their ballots by mail, and nearly half voted before Election Day. And voting by mail is not just something we did during Covid and then completely abandoned like wiping down our groceries or thanking first responders. Early voting and vote by mail have expanded access to the ballot box, making it easier for more Americans to participate in the electoral process, including:

- ☑ People who have disabilities or mobility issues and can't travel to their polling places

- ☑ Anyone working an hourly job with no paid time off who would otherwise have to choose between casting their vote and earning a paycheck

- ☑ Parents and caretakers who are unable to show up on Election Day because they have to take care of a sick relative or a child who got into the Halloween candy and is bouncing off the walls

- ☑ Students at college out of state or who are studying abroad to find themselves . . . a ripped Australian guy

There are a lot of benefits to voting early or by mail. You can take time to fill out your ballot and look up anyone or anything you find confusing. One other plus – the sooner you vote, the sooner you can tell a campaign you voted when they text or call you, which means the sooner they will leave you alone. And by casting your ballot early, you are also helping campaigns figure out which voters they still need to reach before Election Day (i.e., not you!).

Do Your Own Research

Voting involves more than just picking your favorite candidates. You have to immerse yourself in local issues, ballot initiatives, and referendums – which are often confusing on purpose in the hope that you might accidentally vote the wrong way. Which is yet another reason to take that extra time with your ballot and vote early.

Here's a little test of your election reading comprehension.

PROP QUIZ

This is the abortion measure that was on the ballot in Kansas in 2022. Can you tell which answer means you're in favor of protecting reproductive rights?

---

§ 22. Regulation of abortion.
Because Kansans value both women and children, the constitution of the state of Kansas does not require government funding of abortion and does not create or secure a right to abortion. To the extent permitted by the constitution of the United States, the people, through their elected state representatives and state senators, may pass laws regarding abortion, including, but not limited to, laws that account for circumstances of pregnancy resulting from rape or incest, or circumstances of necessity to save the life of the mother.

○ **Yes**
○ **No**

And as if that wasn't dense enough, ballots often include a lengthy explainer to go along with each measure, like this one:

Question Submitted

Constitutional Amendment

Vote Yes or No

Explanatory statement. The Value Them Both Amendment would affirm there is no Kansas constitutional right to abortion or to require the government funding of abortion, including, but not limited to, in circumstances of pregnancy resulting from rape or incest, or when necessary to save the life of the mother.

A vote **for** the Value Them Both Amendment would affirm there is no Kansas constitutional right to abortion or to require the government funding of abortion and would reserve to the people of Kansas, through their elected state legislators, the right to pass laws to regulate abortion.

The vote **against** the Value Them Both Amendment would make no changes to the constitution of the state of Kansas, and could restrict the people, through their elected state legislators, from regulating abortion by leaving in place the recently recognized rights to abortion.

Shall the following be adopted?

Some ballot propositions address pressing matters of the day. Others do not. In many states, if you have the drive to collect enough signatures, you can get all kinds of crazy shit on the ballot. And we made a game out of that!

MAD PROPS

Here's how this game works: we will present a ballot measure, and you have to guess whether it's real (R) or fake (F). (Answers provided at the bottom.)

1. Arizona once had a failed ballot measure that asked whether one random voter should get $1 million after every general election.

2. In response to those popular Pace Picante Sauce commercials in the '90s, the city of San Antonio passed an ordinance banning the sale of any salsa made in New York City.

3. San Francisco approved a measure that would allow a local police officer to go on patrol accompanied by his ventriloquist dummy, Brendan O'Smarty.

4. Florida is currently considering a new law that would implement a "substitution tax" for anyone from "out of state" who tries to make substitutions when ordering at a diner.

5. In 2012, the town of Idyllwild, California, elected a feral cat as mayor.

With so many puzzling items on the ballot, you may also want to consult a voter guide. For example, just off the top of our heads, this is a pretty great one: **votesaveamerica.com**

Election Day Essentials

Let's assume that you've decided to vote in person on Election Day. Maybe your ballot got lost. Maybe you're old-school. Maybe you're a messy bitch who lives for drama. Or maybe you just forgot. It's all fine! You're doing it.

Here are some key items you may want to bring with you in case there's a line . . .

- Snacks.

- Water.

- One of those portable phone charging batteries, in case you need it, or (and this could happen) a hot person is behind you and he says "Oh shit my phone's almost dead" like to himself and you say "Oh sorry, didn't mean to eavesdrop, but do you need a phone charger?" and then he says "Oh wow thanks" and then you say "Come here often?" And then he says "What?" and takes out an AirPod, and then you say "Oh never mind, sorry, I said 'Come here often?'" and he says "Oh, ha, right." And you say "Because it's a presidential election so of course we don't come here often but anyway enjoy the juice." And then you think about how you said the word "juice" which is so weird and you become a dead voter right there on the spot.

Watch out for scams. If you get a letter or a robocall telling you to vote on the wrong day – it's fake. Also, just to be safe, at this point assume all phone calls are fake. Your mother calling and asking for the last four digits of your social? Scam alert. Your ex-girlfriend calling to say she still loves you, a hope you've carried for years in your lonely beating heart? Scam alert.

Oh, and one important reminder: don't forget to take and post a photo of yourself with your "I voted" sticker. That's a big part of the experience. If you don't post, how will anyone ever know that you're a good person? They simply won't.

Election Day/Week/Month

One side effect of the recent surge in voting by mail is that it often leads to delayed results. In states like Arizona and California it can take several days for the full tally, which can be very frustrating for voters and Steve Kornacki. Election night has turned into election week (but oh, the suspense!) In 2018, it seemed like Kyrsten Sinema and most of the Democrats running for House seats in Southern California had lost – until all the mail-in ballots were counted. And of course, we all know how that scenario played out in 2020. (Without a hitch!)

As we've seen over the past few cycles, elections don't always go the way you expect – so it's a good idea to brace yourself for the worst.

THE BEST PLACES TO SCREAM INTO THE VOID

Well, you did it. You cast your vote. Now get back in line and do it all over again in every local and national election for the rest of your life.

What Have We Learned?

- There are no off years
- votesaveamerica.com
- The CIA killed JFK because he was too hot

Step 4

THE BUCK STARTS HERE

SO YOU VOTED, and maybe your preferred candidate won in a landslide. Huzzah! Or maybe she lost to a CrossFit instructor who stormed the Capitol. It happens! Next election, it's time to think outside the ballot box – and support your candidate with more than a vote.

This chapter will focus on the dos and don'ts of donating – investing your own money in the candidates and causes you believe in while navigating America's deeply fucked campaign finance system. (Side note: if you are a pro-democracy billionaire with a Hungarian accent who happens to be reading this, skip to the next section – this isn't for you.)

Big Money, Big Problems

Election season is that magical time when candidates inspire us to open our hearts, our minds, and our wallets. American elections are a booming industry. According to the research group OpenSecrets, a record $14.4 billion was spent on the 2020 election, and 2024 will probably turn out to be even more expensive. Money is flowing through our political system like never before – thanks at least in part to the five Supreme Court justices who opened their robes in 2010 to piss on a century of campaign finance reforms in a case called . . .

Citizens United

You've heard of it and even blamed it for a lot of our problems in casual conversation, but now it's time to find out what *Citizens United* is. Essentially, the Supreme Court ruled that limiting the amount a corporation can spend on elections would be a violation of free speech. So now corporations and outside groups can spend however much they want in support of a candidate as long as they don't directly give that money to the candidate or their party.

Super PACs

Whereas a mere mortal political action committee can only accept $5,000 per year from individuals, super PACs are able to raise unlimited funds from individuals or corporations. What makes them so super? Well, they can run ads, hire field organizers, and basically do the work of a campaign. (Ron DeSantis outsourced almost everything to his super

PAC, and boy did it deliver!) The only real restriction is that super PACs cannot coordinate *with* or directly give money *to* the actual campaign. Many of these super PACs are advocates for major candidates or issues – others are just dumb. Here are some names of actual super PACs that have popped up over the years: Americans for More Rhombus, Raptors for Jesus, Zombies of Tomorrow, Bearded Entrepreneurs for the Advancement of a Responsible Democracy, or BEARD. It's crazy to think Americans could get more rhombus before we get more gun laws. What a gloriously stupid time to be alive. Election spending via super PACs has skyrocketed in recent years, giving massive influence over our elections to a handful of wealthy Americans. Also known as . . .

Megadonors

If elections are a casino, these are the high rollers getting their rooms comped and smoking Cohibas. (Also, several megadonors have owned casinos!) Since 2009, they have spent billions on elections. In the 2022 cycle, the top ten heaviest hitters combined to drop more than $415 million. These megadonors get their calls returned, their meetings taken, their ideas heard, their pet projects funded, their job candidates placed, and their dreams of becoming the ambassador to some tropical island fulfilled. They exert considerably more influence on our politics than 99.9 percent of Americans. But are they happy?

Dark Money

Are you a *low-key* billionaire who loves influencing political outcomes but hates the pesky disclosure requirements that come with donating directly to candidates or their super PACs? Well, then you're going to love dark money! Thanks to the Supreme Court, people can essentially give unlimited amounts of money to, among other entities, nonprofit "social welfare" organizations that don't have to publicly disclose their donors. More than a billion dollars was spent by dark money groups that masked the identities of their donors in the 2020 federal election cycle alone. It's the human centipede of corporate money and terrible policy outcomes and we're the caboose.

Why does big money matter so much? Because all those campaign ads and billboards and emails and phone calls and flyers shoved under your door – they work! In the last mid-term, the higher-spending Senate candidate won 82 percent of races, while the higher-spending House candidate won a staggering 93 percent of the time. Bad news: we are not going to overturn *Citizens United* or change the campaign finance laws overnight. Good news: if we all donate what we can afford, we can stop the megadonors from drowning out our candidates and causes.

The Grassroots Is Sometimes Greener

The internet has made it easier than ever for candidates to raise a lot of money from a big, broad base of supporters. That means candidates don't have to spend all their time begging for money at events with wealthy donors who ask, "What's *our* version of Make America Great Again?" It also makes candidates more accountable to the people who elect them. After all, if a candidate gets most of their funds from moguls and corporations, who do you think their policies are more likely to benefit? But if a candidate gets a million dollars from 100,000 different donors, it dilutes the influence of big money. Plus, more donors means more people who can volunteer and spread the word about a campaign.

And if you're looking for some extra credit, make a recurring small-dollar donation. Campaigns are better equipped to plan for the future when they have a reliable source of cash. Yes, a small recurring donation is more of a commitment. But consider this: you can have a real and lasting impact on the outcome of an election for less than the price of your most obnoxious friend's Patreon (you know who you are, Devin).

One of the early success stories involving small-dollar donations was the Obama campaign. The conventional wisdom at the time was that when it came to raising money, there was no way Obama could compete with established candidates like Hillary Clinton (whom one of us thinks is perfect) and John McCain (loved his later stuff, like saving Obamacare). He was too new to politics, and their donor lists were too deep. Then Obama raised $745 million in the 2008 cycle. How? He definitely had to schmooze many a rich person, but he also raised a lot of money in small donations through the internet and huge fundraising events that were more like grassroots rallies. By the end of 2012, Obama had raised over $1.1 billion (including $234 million in small-dollar donations). By the way, Donald Trump also used the same playbook to great effect.

Online donations, like most things in politics, can cut both ways. Is it good for the republic that a presidential candidate can raise millions of dollars online every time he's indicted? Absolutely not. Do we love that online fundraising incentivizes campaigns to gin up outrage with apocalyptic language that further poisons our political climate? We don't! But small-dollar donations have helped little-known outsiders prevail against establishment candidates when a few decades ago they might not have been able to raise the money necessary to compete.

Show Me the Small Money!

OK – so you've decided to spend some of your hard-earned paycheck or the modest inheritance from your great aunt to help win elections, but you made the mistake of giving your email address to a Democratic candidate, which means that now every Democrat running for office is hitting you up with the most annoying texts and emails of all time. Unless . . . maybe . . . Hakeem Jeffries really *does* want to know if you've seen the latest CNN poll that shows Republicans pulling ahead in the generic ballot? Anyway, now you have to figure out how to get the biggest bang for your buck.

Which Candidates and Campaigns Are Really Worth It?

Maybe a candidate inspired you so hard that your Apple Pay just started firing off donations from your pocket. If that's the case, how nice for you. Being inspired by a candidate is a great reason to support a campaign. But so is cold, hard *Moneyball* shit. We need to use our limited resources to put our candidates in the best position to win. Before you dip into your savings, ask yourself a couple of basic questions: Did this person make a viral video about running against one of the biggest assholes in Congress? Also, and this is slightly more important: Do they actually have a chance of winning?

Take the 2020 Senate map for example. There was a grassroots effort in Kentucky to defeat Senate Majority Leader Mitch McConnell. And boy, was it exciting! It's fun to get behind a scrappy, energetic campaign taking on one of America's worst grandpas. But in the end, Democrats spent more than $90 million in The Bluegrass State, and McConnell still won by 20 points. Meanwhile, the money we donated to candidates in states like Georgia, Arizona, and Colorado went a hell of a lot further: victories in *those* states meant Democrats took control of the Senate. McConnell may have kept his seat, but lost his job as Majority Leader. And now he's Chuck Schumer's bitch.

The same logic applies in the House. A lot of candidates in long-shot bids will raise money with amazing personal stories, fantastic ads, and by running against top-tier schmucks. But some of those schmucks are in R+16 districts. What's an R+16 district? So glad you asked. The Cook Political Report puts out a score for each state and district that shows how partisan a district or state is compared to the country as a whole. A score of R+16, for example, means that over the last two presidential elections, that district was 16 percentage points more Republican than the rest of the country – which means it'll be pretty tough for any Democrat to get elected. That's not to say you should never give to a long-shot candidate – if someone really inspires you, then go for it! Just don't get drawn in by internet hype and claims that your contribution could be the difference against a Republican who won their last election by 45 points. In that scenario, your contribution is far more likely to make campaign consultants rich than sway an election. The way to make the other side hurt is to hit 'em in the races where they can actually lose seats. A rating of R+5 or less? Very doable! A race that's rated a toss-up or even a slight Republican lean? Get in there!

You might be wondering: How do I find those races? Don't worry, we've got you covered. Way back in 2018, we created *Vote Save America* as a one-stop shop for information about where to donate and how to register, volunteer, and figure out who and what is on your ballot. Since we launched *Vote Save America*, people have donated more than $55 million to help flip the House in 2018, take back the White House and Senate in 2020, beat back the red wave in 2022, and elect pro-choice, pro-democracy candidates at every level. Our volunteers also registered hundreds of thousands of voters and sent millions of annoying/inspiring texts and phone calls.

You also need to make sure your money is actually going to the person you're sending it to. Avoid scams where your dollars go to another candidate or some third-party group you've never heard of. For example, in 2022, Donald Trump's Save America PAC sent a fundraising email on behalf of Georgia Senate hopeful Herschel Walker. But when you looked at the fine print, it revealed that Trump's PAC was keeping 90 percent of the contributions. Which wasn't cool. That money was meant for a different asshole!

Oh, another important question . . . How desperate does the candidate seem? Is he humbly asking or pathetically begging in ALL CAPS AND A GENEROUS FONT SIZE?

These are immediate red flags of emails to ignore:

- Nancy Pelosi is FED UP!

- On the verge of literal tears

- URGENT

- Sobbing in the bathroom and my campaign manager is pounding on the door

- I THINK I'M GAY

- HOW MANY TIMES ARE WE GOING TO HAVE TO ASK, TOMMY?

- Our records show your Trump Advisory Board membership status is STILL PENDING ACTIVATION!

- I JUST TOLD MY WIFE I'M GAY

- Is your phone off, patriot?

- Patriot! YOU NEVER ANSWERED YOUR PHONE!

- I AM SENATOR GARY PETERS, AND I AM GAY

And if the fundraising email is from a PAC or nonprofit of some kind . . . ask yourself: What is this organization that's yelling at me from my inbox? Do they have a track record? Or a criminal record? Are they real? Is any of this real? (Nothing is real. Except for us. Except for this.) So to recap: Read the fine print! Where is the money going? Directly to a candidate or cause? Or to Steve Bannon's fake GoFundMe to pay for the wall that got him indicted?

And if you are planning to give, give as early as possible so that your money can be spent on long-term organizing and doesn't just go to extra campaign ads in the final week. The earlier you donate, the better. Think of it like this: You're planning a swanky soiree for Boris Johnson during the height of a massive pandemic. BoJo gave you a budget of 1,000 pounds, but the night before the party you get a donation of 10,000 more pounds. Yes, you can use the money to load up on Yorkshire pudding and double the number of kidney pies, but the caterer can't change the menu that late. Maybe now you can afford that Wham! cover band, but they're already booked. And now you're buggered.

In 2020, a lot of campaigns got donations toward the end of the race, but there were fewer ad spots left to buy, and the money wasn't able to be used efficiently, or even spent at all. In 2004, many Democrats were furious when they learned that John Kerry ended the campaign with more than $15 million in the bank. And yet throughout the campaign, he repeatedly denied Lovett's demands for a raise "commensurate with his talents." (He was an intern.)

And just like we discussed with voting – it's important to contribute beyond those big, shiny national matchups. You get a bigger bang for your buck in local races. They cost less to fund, so the further down the ballot a race is, the further every dollar goes.

And if you ever feel too burdened by the amount of correspondence that's coming your way from a campaign or group – you can always just text "STOP" at any point . . . and the messages will not stop at all.

State Party in the USA!

Don't forget state parties! Well, OK – in some states you can forget the state party because it's not clear that it actually exists. But in other states, like Wisconsin for example, they're doing year-round fundraising, phone banks, door knocking, and voter registration.

★ ASK SOMEONE SMARTER THAN US ★

Ben Wikler

Chair of the Wisconsin Democratic Party, 2020 winner for "State Party of the Year" (*Washington Post*).

Why do state parties need our support?

Donating to state parties is a very high-leverage, high-impact play. You're funding the Get Out the Vote infrastructure that absolutely has to happen in each state. State parties do not have a lot of money to fool around with, and they tend to run lean, high-impact operations.

You can think of candidates as the cars on the roads, and state parties build those roads. A state party that has built a strong infrastructure can make every candidate more effective, and can make it possible to win races that would have otherwise been lost by heartbreaking margins. They can make it possible for people to run for office who otherwise wouldn't be able to, because the state party is running candidate and staff training, can bring together donors and provide financial support for candidates, and do the Get Out the Vote work. They can make the difference in an election. State parties play a behind-the-scenes role in everything from winning presidential elections in a state to winning school board races, county board majorities, and tipping state legislatures. A state party running a year-round organizing operation can turn defeats into opportunities for the next election, and be a bulwark for democracy at a moment when democracy is under threat.

And if you're ever not sure what to do – like we said, there are amazing resources out there, put together by supersmart, widely revered sources. For example:

What Have We Learned?

- Money can buy elections but NOT happiness
- IF YOU DON'T DONATE NOW TO THE HOUSE VICTORY FUND I'LL KILL AGAIN
- Michigan Senator Gary Peters is gay

Step 5

VOLUNTEER

so you just blew your bonus on a hotly contested race for state comptroller, and now you're ready to take your relationship with democracy to the next level. Giving your time to a candidate or campaign can be even more valuable than giving your money. After all, sometimes candidates who are outspent win. Why? Late-breaking sex scandals! But also, volunteers.

We've arrived at the part of your journey where you have to interact with other human beings, whether you like it or not. In this chapter, we'll explore how to successfully reach persuadable voters. Yes, you might have to abandon your comfort zone and break that "no small talk" New Year's resolution, but you are also about to discover that with a little effort, a little homework, and a little compassion – you can actually change minds and get people to the polls.

The Art of Persuasion

You may be under the impression that there aren't many persuadable voters out there, and so there isn't much point in trying to contact voters directly to change their minds. "The juice," you wonder, "is it worth the squeeze?" Yes, America has tens of millions of voters with political beliefs and partisan preferences that rarely change. That's us. That might be you. But most of our fellow citizens aren't nearly as obsessed with politics as we are, and their political views are all over the place. There is a huge number of voters who are undecided about

    (a) who they're voting for

    and

    (b) if they're voting at all.

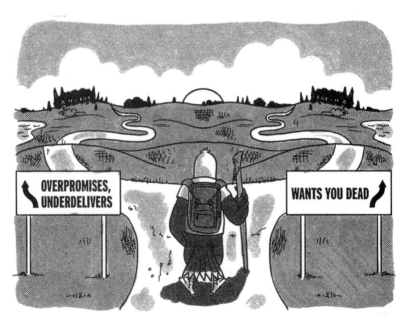

In 2016, about one in eight voters was undecided going into the final week of the campaign. That's more than 12 percent of the electorate up for grabs! According to political scientists Yanna Krupnikov and John Barry Ryan, coauthors of *The Other Divide*, only 15 to 20 percent of Americans pay close attention to politics. And while the other 80 to 85 percent may vote, they aren't chain-smoking campaign updates and getting so obsessive about swing state polling that Chuck Todd has to take out a restraining order.

So what do you do when you come across someone who hasn't yet committed to voting for your candidate of choice? Do you calmly explain that they've been brainwashed? Provide a detailed fact-check? Tell your mom she's a fascist? You can try!

But this isn't the internet, it's real life. Take a quick self-inventory. Have you ever changed your mind about something? And when you did, was it because someone berated you into submission? Of course not. You change your mind like everyone else: you get in a big fight with your spouse while doing the dishes, then two hours later right before bed you say, "Look at us, fighting. It's silly! I'm sorry. And of course I regret becoming a fake elector."

Scolding might be cathartic, and even warranted, but the ultimate goal is not to make you feel better about how right your political views are. That's what social media is for! The goal is to convince others to join your movement or support your candidate so that your political views are ultimately shared by the people who write the laws and run the government.

We heard from an inspiring volunteer named Angela who appeared on another one of our podcasts. She started a chapter of *Indivisible* – a progressive grassroots organization – in a pretty deep-red part of western Pennsylvania, and shared the story of the first time she went canvassing:

> The second door I knocked, it was just a listening
> canvass to talk to people about health care. And the
> woman immediately said, "I don't want to talk to you. I
> voted for Trump, and I don't want to be talked out of it."
> And instead of just walking away, we started talking. I
> said, "I'm just out here today because I'm scared. I have
> MS, my medicine costs eight thousand dollars a month,
> and I don't know what I'd do without insurance." And

so we slowly started talking. We ended up talking for 15 minutes. And turns out she's terrified about the cost of drugs too. And she thinks it's corrupt, and she feels like politicians care more about the drug companies than they do about us. And by the end of it, she thanked me for going out there: "Well, thank you for the work you're doing." We just talked as humans. We got to see that it's not us and them – Democrat, Republican – it's us and them, the people versus the very powerful few.

———

We often focus a lot on how polarized we are (because we are), but for all our many differences of opinion, a majority of Americans actually agree on a lot.

- According to a 2023 Gallup poll, 71 percent of Americans think same-sex marriage should be legal. In 1996, that number was only 27 percent.

- 59 percent of Americans opposed the decision to overturn *Roe v. Wade*, and according to a 2023 *USA Today* poll, 80 percent of Americans oppose a federal abortion ban.

- A poll in 2023 found at least 80 percent of registered voters favor mandating criminal background checks and mental health checks for gun buyers, enforcing current gun laws more effectively, making 21 the minimum age to purchase a gun, and letting police temporarily take guns away from people who may be dangerous. And that's a poll from Fox News!

- According to a 2023 CNN Poll, 73 percent of American adults say the US government should "develop its climate policies with the goal of cutting the country's planet-warming pollution in half by the end of the decade."

The fact that a majority of Americans have come to share these views should give you a little boost of confidence as you have conversations when you phone bank and knock on doors. And to make it easier for volunteers, a lot of campaigns have access to data that helps identify the most persuadable undecided voters. As you start talking to some of these voters, you'll encounter a surprisingly diverse group of people with views that are a mix of complicated, confusing, contradictory, and just sort of weird. Like the registered independent who loves Bernie Sanders and Medicare for All but voted for Trump as an "outsider" to change Washington. Or the 30-something tech bro who voted for Obama but did an entire podcast episode about why *Barbie* is an attack on men and Taiwan's sovereignty. And of course, you'll still get plenty of colorful characters who will ask you if you've ever met the body double who replaced Hillary Clinton (we have, she's so nice). The key is to separate the persuadables from the diehards.

Research shows that Americans are more receptive to information about politics from people they trust. Which begs the eternal question: Do you speak up when your sister's second husband expresses yet another dogshit political opinion at this godforsaken gender reveal? Or do you let it go? You can do whatever. No one gets into heaven for arguing at a wedding, and no one goes to hell because they kept it chill at a bar mitzvah.

It may or may not be worth it to really dig in with your MAGA father-in-law about how pronouns were invented by antifa to cancel straight white men. But at the very least, it's worth checking in with your cousin who voted for Jill Stein when they were living in Brooklyn but who just moved to Atlanta. Even more worthwhile: getting a friend in a swing state who shares most of your political views but not your political obsession to vote. That way you can cancel the vote of one of those MAGA-boat people without ever having to hear what that person thinks about AOC (he secretly loves her).

———

Alexandria Ocasio-Cortez

How to reach non-voters

One of the biggest misconceptions that we have in politics is that people who don't vote are apathetic. And if anything, sometimes I find them to be the most passionate about politics. And they're just very heartbroken and dejected. The only way you are going to get those voters is by actually telling the truth.

The truth is, most Americans either don't vote or don't vote for only one party. If we can persuade just a fraction of those people to change their minds, it can change the outcome of an election. Of course, it's not easy to get people to vote for the other party. And by the way, it's also not easy to get infrequent voters to actually cast their ballots (even though they tend to be younger, they also tend to be more moderate, apolitical, and have strong feelings about not voting). But both things are absolutely possible. You just have to know what to expect.

From infrequent voters, you may hear, "All politicians are corrupt and useless, nothing changes, don't waste my time." And while that's frustrating and self-fulfilling at times, for people who haven't felt politics make a difference in their lives, it's understandable. And who are you to tell them they're wrong? You majored in theater.

So how do we get them to vote?

- Ask about the issues they care about the most and point out the difference between both parties on those issues.

- Respect their experiences and points of view.

- Talk specifically about how their lives would change depending on which party wins.

- Remind them that if they don't vote, huge decisions that affect their lives and the lives of their families will be made by a bunch of assholes they've never met.

- Casually mention that the most cynical and corrupt people in politics are the ones who want you to vote the least.

- Lose your patience and scream, "You keep saying you don't know what these politicians are for but . . . look it up maybe? I'm sorry, I don't mean to shout and your concerns are valid, but can I borrow your phone and subscribe to a newsletter for you or something? He tried to hang his own vice president!"

Barack Obama

Obama's GOTV message

On every issue that young people in particular care about, let's stipulate that the government's not gonna solve every problem overnight. But you know what? It can make it better. And better means lives saved. Better means the air is a little less polluted. Better means that maybe some people don't get charged for crimes that they shouldn't be charged for. And some people don't get shot. That's worth fighting for. And the idea that you'd give away your power because you're not getting 100 percent when you could get 30 percent, 40 percent, 50 percent better, that doesn't make any sense. Don't let the best be the enemy of the good in this situation. There are constraints in our system. Even a well-meaning president can't solve everything. But they can make some things better.

Part of the challenge will be to combat the growing sense from the "RFK Jr. makes some great points" crowd that being passionate or hopeful about politics is loser shit, and that pessimism and indifference are how to prove you get what's *really* going on. The best way to break through that wall of apathy and doom is to make the stakes of every election as personal as possible. For instance:

"Do you have a relative with a preexisting medical condition who's worried they might lose their health insurance if

Congress tries to repeal the Affordable Care Act for the 500th time?"

"Do you believe you should be in charge of your own physical body instead of a hyper-religious lawyer who wants to be president one day?"

"Do you have a lesbian cousin who is anxious about living in a state where they passed a 'Don't Say Gay' law because she teaches high school seniors and in May when they all emotionally check out, she plans to say, 'Screw it' and make them watch *Angels in America* for a week?"

The Volun-Tiers

These are a few of the ways you can swing voters toward a candidate you are passionate about. We've listed the following volunteer activities in order from those that require the least contact to those that require the most.

Postcards

Are you an unemployed screenwriter? A bored grandma? You're gonna crush it at writing postcards. This is probably the most low-key way to reach voters who still open their mail and read letters from strangers. But hey, if this is all you've got the bandwidth for, we'll take it!

WHAT TO EXPECT: Honestly, not too much. You get a list of names and addresses, handwrite some postcards, and that's that. But have fun with it. Be creative. Draw some smiley faces and shit.

IDEAL OUTCOME: A voter reads your postcard then uses it as a coaster for a beer. Or maybe the mailman looks at your postcard as he delivers it and remembers to vote, then the woman you mailed it to also looks at it and remembers to vote. And immediately calls five of her friends to remind them also to vote.

WORST-CASE SCENARIO: Your postcard is misread by a jealous and paranoid husband convinced his wife is having a torrid love affair with a Democrat in Chevy Chase, Maryland.

Text Banking

For all of you aspiring shut-ins out there. This is where you reach out to voters via text to remind them to register, vote, or sign up to volunteer. Text banking has been proven to increase turnout by 1 to 2 percent. Which is great! That's the strength of an effective hydrocortisone cream AND enough to make the difference in a lot of races.

WHAT TO EXPECT: Getting thousands of texts that say "STOP."

IDEAL OUTCOME: You have a meaningful conversation with an undecided voter, or you remind someone that it's the last day they can register to vote – all without ever having to talk on the phone. Ideas are shared, views are shifted, a voting plan is scheduled, emojis are exchanged.

WORST-CASE SCENARIO: Accidentally send a selfie from the toilet.

Phone Banking

Are you an extrovert who's out of clean clothes? Time for some phone banking. Basically, you dial away and chat it up with voters until you can't take it anymore.

WHAT TO EXPECT: No one answers the phone these days.

IDEAL OUTCOME: A lengthy dialogue with an undecided voter that reaffirms your faith in democracy.

WORST-CASE SCENARIO: A lengthy dialogue with an undecided voter that shatters your faith in democracy.

Get Out the Vietor

In 2002, I got my first campaign job – a three-week stint in North Carolina doing Get Out the Vote for Erskine Bowles's Senate campaign against Elizabeth Dole. After a brief meeting with Erskine's campaign team, a couple of us new recruits were dispatched to Buncombe County, which is in the far western corner of the state at the foot of the Blue Ridge Mountains. I stayed on some person's couch and worked out of the local Democratic Party office. We knocked on doors during the day and made GOTV calls at night. When the calls started to feel tedious, we would make up fake names or try to get through a full script doing an accent. By Election Day, my southern dialect was halfway decent, and I had successfully placed hundreds of GOTV calls as "Jackson Jessup."

And for the more adventurous volunteer . . .

Canvassing

Do you know how to calm a suspicious pit bull? Canvassing could be right for you! Ideally, canvassing involves knocking on doors for an election that's happening in your state, or even in your community – talking to friends and neighbors is the most effective method of persuasion. And it can boost turnout by 5 to 10 percent! But sometimes, the bigger campaigns in need of volunteers will send you to a neighborhood you've never been to, in a state where you don't live, to knock on strangers' doors. (Fun? Fun!)

WHAT TO EXPECT: Most people will not be home, even though every light in their house and their TV is on.

IDEAL OUTCOME: You have a lively back-and-forth that results in someone making a plan or deciding to vote for your candidate.

WORST-CASE SCENARIO: You fall in love . . . with being told to fuck off.

We have spent countless hours door knocking over the past two decades, and here are some tips we've picked up that might serve you well out there.

- Bring a friend. Canvassing is much more fun with a buddy.

- View every single voter interaction, even the ones that start poorly, as an opportunity. Don't be too pushy or annoying, but also don't be easily scared away – you have to put some real effort into getting voters to talk with you. It can be awkward! But even if someone blows you off or slams the door in your face (which is highly likely), always be polite and thank them for their time. You don't want to end up like that canvasser for Ron DeSantis who got caught on a Ring camera saying a voter should "eat his balls," and then added he was "a little stoned." A little aggro for being stoned if you ask us.

- Ask open-ended questions and *actually listen* to what people say in response. Yes, it's important to talk about your candidate/their policies, but if you just mindlessly spew talking points at people, they will tune you out. It's much more impactful if you can work the campaign messaging into the conversation in response to something a voter tells you. Just be yourself and try to have a genuine back-and-forth about real stuff.

- Record your data! It doesn't matter how many great conversations you have at the door if you don't record the results. The campaign is counting on you to provide an accurate account of every interaction (or noninteraction) you have.

Yes, We Canvass

I spent 2007 in Iowa working on Obama's caucus campaign. My title was Iowa press secretary, which means I traveled with then Senator Obama to nearly all his events, was the day-to-day point of contact for Iowa-based reporters, and feted national media big shots when they swept in and out of town (this often got me dinner on an expense account, which is a nice perk when you're 27 and broke). My boss, our state director, was a guy named Paul Tewes. Paul was (and still is) a brilliant organizer and master motivator. He liked to remind the senior staff in Iowa and visitors from our HQ in Chicago that no job was too big or small for them. That often meant "encouraging" (read: forcing) people like me to knock on doors or make GOTV calls in our free time (note: we had no free time). One day, Paul called the whole Des Moines team together and made all the senior staffers draw from a hat. Inside were locations for canvassing assignments that weekend. As we picked, it soon became clear that Paul had only put border counties in the hat (i.e., places that were as far away from Des Moines as possible). So the next morning, I hopped into my truck and drove to Worth County, a two-hour drive from Des Moines, right on the border of Minnesota. The first few hours were not great. I walked, I knocked, I left campaign literature in doors when no one was home (note: literally no one was home). After a couple hours, I was sweaty, exhausted, and pissed about wasting my time. Just as I was about to give up, I saw a woman on a riding mower. Her address was not on my walk list. I had no idea if she even lived at that house, let alone was a registered voter. But I walked up to her, we started talking, and a few minutes later, I had a "one." That was the code we used for someone who agreed to caucus for Obama and signed a supporter card. I lived in Iowa for an entire year. I went to hundreds of events, worked my ass off, met countless celebrities and surrogates, but that day of canvassing and getting that one supporter card was one of my proudest and most distinct memories from Iowa. (At least until I found myself on Vivek Ramaswamy's campaign bus nearly 20 years later, debating whether January 6th was an inside job.)

───────

You may be intimidated by the thought of door knocking or cold calling. That's perfectly normal. It's an unglamorous activity with an uncertain outcome. Also, the idea of human contact fills some people with dread. When you spend an hour phone banking and only reach one real person, it's understandable to feel like you're not making much of an impact. But here's what you have to remember: First, you're part of a team. At scale, hundreds of people like you knocking on doors and making calls adds up fast and *will* make a difference. Once you get offline, people are a lot nicer and open-minded. Who knew? (Our parents, who got to live before the internet.)

Volunteers are especially important in downballot races. Smaller campaigns have smaller budgets for ads and billboards, so reaching out to people directly can have a huge impact in those elections. And while direct contact with voters can be super helpful, it's not the only way to get involved with a campaign. If hitting the phones and banging down doors isn't right for you, that's also fine. There are plenty of opportunities to maximize your talents. Are you tech savvy? Can you hack a DNC server? Are you good at graphic design? Can you juggle? Put the "special skills" on your resume to use. Also, you know what great volunteers can do? Train other volunteers!

The Weirdest Thing I Ever Did For a Campaign

The first campaign I volunteered on was the 2002 New Hampshire Senate race between then Governor Jeanne Shaheen (D) and then Congressman John Sununu (R). Every day that summer, I'd drive 45 minutes to the Democratic Party HQ in Manchester and do whatever they needed – mostly door knocking, phone banking, and driving the press staff to events, which ultimately led to my proudest moment in politics. The Republicans were running a pretty nasty campaign, even for them (google "2002 New Hampshire Senate election phone-jamming scandal"), and Shaheen's campaign was looking for some press coverage of what they were calling "GOP trash attacks." The stunt they came up with was to cover me in a trash bag, poke a few holes so I could see and breathe, put a sign on me that read, "GOP TRASH ATTACKS," and have me walk out from behind a dumpster in hopes that a local news channel would film it.

And somehow . . . they did! I got home that night just in time to see my big debut on WMUR's evening news. Jeanne Shaheen went on to lose that race, but she won her 2008 Senate race, and because I know how hard my friends have tried to look for it, I'm fairly certain that WMUR has deleted the footage – so, in the end, everyone wins!

———

All politics aside, the best part of volunteering on a campaign is that you get to do it with other people who share your values and sense of purpose. It's not just about whether your candidate wins or loses – it's about the friendships you make along the way (but mostly, it's about whether your candidate wins or loses).

What Have We Learned?

- While canvassing, you will be told to fuck off more times than Cousin Greg

- If you have access to the WMUR news footage of Favs in a trash bag, put this book down and upload it to YouTube immediately

- Still undecided? He tried to hang his own vice president

Step 6

ORGANIZE

OK – NOW YOU'RE really in it. You helped a grandmother in Grand Rapids "make a plan," you spent 40 minutes on the phone trying to convince a microdosing advocate in Colorado Springs that Tuesday is the day that comes after Monday and before Wednesday. But you're ready for a new challenge. Perhaps you've noticed a flickering streetlamp near your house that's creating a rave-like atmosphere and attracting unruly teens. So what do you do? You become the person who tries to get that streetlamp fixed. Through your participation thus far, you have invested emotionally (and financially!) in putting like-minded candidates in office who pledged to pursue policies that you support. But what if your candidate turned out to be some freak? Or what if you've elected friggin' Malala, but she doesn't have the votes to pass her agenda? What do you do then? Eat shit? No, you get to work.

Organizers don't wait. They understand that in order to fix that streetlamp (and everything else), voting is necessary, but not sufficient. It's tempting to view politics as a transaction: we give candidates our vote, and in return, they solve all our problems while we try new restaurants until the next election. And that would be nice! Unfortunately, that's not how democracy in a country of 300 million people works – especially when a lot of those people are super annoying.

A healthy, functioning democracy requires all of us to be involved all the goddamn time. And yes, we all have jobs and responsibilities and new episodes of *Selling Sunset* to catch up on, but the alternative here is . . . Well, we're living in it, babe. We know the prospect of organizing others (let alone yourself!) is daunting. As you learned out in the field, persuasion is hard. But when more people get involved in more places, more than just a few weeks a year right before a national election, good stuff happens! So in this chapter, we're gonna help you turn your relationship with democracy from a *hobby* into a *habit* (←Lovett once pitched that line to Hillary). Mere pages from now, you'll have the organizational skills to create change within your community and beyond.

Am I Already an Organizer?

Some of you may be thinking, "I never miss my Maddow, I have one of those 'In This House' signs on my front lawn, I've still got a faded 'Feel the Bern' sticker on my laptop . . . I'm already an activist!" Good for you, but that's not quite enough. Lots of people believe they're actively engaged in politics, when in fact, they're not.

FIVE ACTS THAT DON'T COUNT AS ACTIVISM

1. Posting "I stand with my INSERT GROUP HERE friends" on Instagram

2. Sharing a *Handmaid's Tale* meme after a controversial abortion ruling

3. Honking your horn while driving past the Women's March

4. Yelling at your dad for watching *Gutfeld!*

5. Showing up to the strike for 20 minutes, taking a selfie and tagging it "#unionstrong," then going to lunch, Lovett

Stacey Abrams

On accountability

We have to be held accountable not only when you vote but when we're in office. And that responsibility rests on the politician to communicate what's happening and why and how. But it also rests on the voters and the citizens to push back and say, "What have you done? Have you done enough, and how can I help?" I say that politicians are like 15-year-olds. We respond to money, peer pressure, and attention. And the responsibility we have is that we need to make sure all three levers are working to make our system better.

So What *Is* Organizing?

Organizing is getting a group of people to take direct action with the purpose of achieving a shared political goal. As an example, let's return to the most important issue of our time: that lamp on your street. Organizing is bringing some of your neighbors to the next city council meeting to demand that your representatives fix the lamp. If that doesn't work, organizing could mean staging a protest outside of city hall, or starting a nonprofit to raise awareness about rave-like streetlamps so that more people see the light (sorry) and join the fight. Maybe the city council said there's not enough money to replace all those blinking bulbs, so you put those canvassing skills to work and get enough signatures for a ballot measure that would raise more revenue. And if all that fails, and you come to the unfortunate realization that the entire city council is in the pocket of Big Rave, you organize a campaign to elect a new one.

Why Organizing Matters

If we only get involved in electoral politics, the only impact we'll ever have is through electing politicians. And because even the best politicians are human, and the worst politicians rarely are, disappointment abounds. Year-round organizing allows us to not only keep the pressure on politicians to do what they promised, it helps to shift public opinion on causes we care about. Instead of only showing up at people's doors to ask for their votes, organizing allows us to have conversations that can change minds and inspire others to get involved. This kind of grassroots organizing can take years to pay off, but it's how meaningful progress is often made. And history is filled with examples – from the women's suffrage movement and the civil rights movement to ballot measures in just the last few years that raised the minimum wage in some pretty red states. Though it's worth remembering: while organizing is why we have things like weekends, lesbian weddings, and rivers that catch fire way less than they did in the 1960s, it's also a tool conservatives deployed over decades to overturn *Roe v. Wade* – another reason we can't afford to just sit on the sidelines.

Maxwell Frost

Former National Organizing Director at March for Our Lives, former National Organizing Specialist for the ACLU, and the first member of Gen Z elected to Congress.

What does it take to become a successful organizer?

Organizing is about connecting with people in your immediate space and giving them an opportunity to be a part of something bigger than themselves, whether it's for a night or a longer struggle. And that's really why organizing is so important. It's how we build power. It's how we use power. It's how we hold power accountable. And it really is the primary tool we have to effect any change in this country.

I've had the privilege of being a part of different struggles. I've been at the 7-Eleven with a clipboard registering voters. I've done the tailgates, registering voters. I have knocked on doors. And I've organized to elect people, including myself. I've also organized direct action on the streets where I've been teargassed, maced, and jailed for it. So as someone who's been a part of a lot of it, I have to say we need it all.

I always tell people a good place to start is to think of an issue that you really care about. Look around because people have been doing this work in your community for a long time. If there's organizing that aligns with your values, and is a safe and healthy

place, then join that organization. Organizing isn't
something that you just start and you're amazing at.
It's like anything else – you've got to practice. You've got
to figure out what you can learn and how you could do
better. And that's how you're going to become a great
organizer.

Ways to Organize

Join a Grassroots Organization

There are so many great nonprofits doing amazing work.
Connecting with a group that has a strong background on an
issue that's important to you is a solid place to start. You'll meet
some very cool people (and some . . . other people) who share
your views. And if no such organization exists, create your
own. Who among us hasn't dreamed of founding a 501(c)(3)
organization? At *Vote Save America*, we work with some fantastic grassroots groups.

Register Voters

This is an ongoing project and takes a lot of people working
diligently and thoroughly year-round. The sooner you register
voters ahead of an election, the sooner they are engaged in the
process and can even help to register others. Again, *Vote Save
America* can help you with that.

Join a Union

As of 2023, 10 percent of American workers were currently members of a labor union, which was less than half of what it was 40 years ago. Volunteering with the local chapter of your union (if you're in one or have a chance to join one) is a great way to organize around issues that directly impact you and your colleagues. And if your workplace doesn't have a union, and you see a colleague pissing into an empty water bottle instead of taking a break so they don't get replaced by a sentient Roomba, you could consider organizing one yourself. Unions can raise wages by up to 15 percent, improve benefits, and have sweeping impact beyond any one company; if a union demands safer working conditions, for example, that can put pressure on a whole industry.

Work with Local Political Parties

Some local parties are run by amazing, dedicated, civic-minded people. Others are run by not enough of those people, and could really use your help. There are plenty of ways to get your foot in the door. And corruption sting operations by the FBI are creating new job openings in party offices all the time.

Ben Wikler

On working with your state party

Another thing you can do with your state party
is to join it. In most states, you can register
to vote as a Democrat, but that doesn't mean
you've joined the Democratic Party. Go to your
state party's website, sign up, join, you'll join
your county party, start going to county party
meetings, and get involved at a local level. You'll
be amazed at how hands-on you can be. County
party tends to be the jumping-off point for people
running for city council, school board, county
board, mayor, and then for Congress and the
state legislature, and ultimately for statewide and
national office.

Most states have fewer than five staff on the
state-party payroll, which means the opportunity
for change is enormous if you get involved in your
state and local Democratic Party. It's low-hanging
fruit, and all you need is the will to get involved,
some extra time, and elbow grease.

Something That Happened

I volunteered at the Nassau County Democratic HQ on Long Island when I was in high school. It was in a nondescript office building. I made and handed out flyers for local candidates, went on errands, broke a copier, made calls to voters, got to meet Hillary Clinton when she was campaigning for Senate years before I worked for her, hung out with some real wackadoos, learned a lot, and had a great time. Local politics isn't as abstract as national politics. It's often pretty transactional and at times a little sleazy (the previous party chair was convicted of fraud, oops), but it's also tangible, personal, and real.

———

Attend a Town Hall, City Council, or School Board Meeting

One of our oldest forums for civic debate and for finding out that a woman you frequently see at the grocery store is getting divorced even though there's no reason for her to mention it during a zoning meeting for the new CVS. Organizing and mobilizing constituents to speak up at these events can shape local policy. But school board meetings and city council sessions are only as valuable and positive as the people who show up. Is it you fighting for a new stop sign? Or is it a Facebook busybody worried that Boo Radley is queer coded?

Don't ever let the kooks in your community deter you from stepping up to the podium. If you want to drive those electric scooters out of your town once and for all because you hate fun, kids, and/or head injuries, making your voice heard at a local meeting is one of the most accessible and effective ways you can appeal to the officials you helped elect.

FIVE TIPS FOR SPEAKING COHERENTLY AT A LOCAL MEETING

1. Avoid references to the microchip Bill Gates installed in your arm.

2. No matter how racy that book at your son's middle school was, please refrain from doing a dramatic reading of the excerpt you found to be the most inappropriate.

3. If you find yourself shouting about a city planner's alcoholism in regard to the need for a speed hump by the YMCA, perhaps you're too close to the issue.

4. Don't present yourself as a medical authority if your degree is in music appreciation.

5. Even if you have the best of intentions . . . never, ever quote Hitler.

And remember: there's a reason they're called "prepared remarks." You have to actually prepare them. The more prepared you are, the more likely your speech could have an impact. Be clear and specific about what you're there to address and keep your remarks brief. They may give you five minutes, but everyone will like you a lot more if you only use two of them. Think about every wedding you've been to – has anyone ever said, "That toast could've used a couple more inside jokes about the groom's fraternity?" It's also a good idea to research the rules and schedule in advance because how and when the public is allowed to participate can vary, and some places require you to sign up for a speaking slot ahead of time. The only thing more stressful than public speaking is finding out at the last minute that you're not allowed to.

★ ASK SOMEONE SMARTER THAN US ★

LaTosha Brown

On building community power

We, quite frankly, got tired of looking at the news and not hearing a lot about Black voters, or if we did hear about Black voters, we were always kind of victimized. It was presented like we didn't have any power. And particularly if you lived in the South, you lived in this red state and you didn't have power or any voice. So we wanted to shift that whole narrative. Black voters matter, we have power, we have influence. And we not only have the power to make America better for ourselves, but for everybody.

Call Your Congressperson

Members of the House have to get re-elected every two years, and really do care about what voters in their districts think. That's why you should call them! Yes, you will probably get connected with an intern, but that intern is logging what you say, and most offices provide the boss with a detailed breakdown of what they're hearing on the phones on a daily or weekly basis. Note that if you are calling from out of district, the member will care a lot less about what you have to say (unless you live in Iowa or New Hampshire since all these people look in the mirror and see a future president). FYI: the phone number for the main switchboard at the Capitol is (202) 224-3121.

Lobby Your Congressperson

Go to Washington and ask for a meeting with your representative or someone in their office. If they refuse to meet, sit outside their office until one of their staffers comes out and offers to schedule a meeting. If that doesn't work, wait for your member to walk out of their office and chase them down as they try to flee into an elevator as the doors are closing. (Extra credit if you record that exchange on your phone.) Dress professionally unless you're John Fetterman, be polite, and if you find yourself going on at length about your mother's plantar fasciitis, find a period on that sentence and bid the legislator adieu.

Form a Private Militia and Plot to Kidnap the Governor of Michigan

Sure, it's a little risky, but what a great story to one day tell your future cellmate.

Boycott

Has the Cracker Barrel gone too woke for your taste? Is Taco Bell refusing to budge on the meat-cheese placement? Maybe a boycott is in order! History is filled with stories of inspiring boycotts – Rosa Parks, Cesar Chavez, the time Sean Hannity convinced viewers to throw their coffee makers out the window.

Like everything else in politics, boycotts have become a bit dumber in recent years. In 2016, Trump supporters called for a boycott of the musical *Hamilton* because during the curtain call, one of the actors delivered a politically charged message to Mike Pence, who was in the audience that night. Did it work? Well, turns out it's hard for Republicans to boycott a show that liberals sold out for the next five years. But hey, in 2021, when Mike Pence refused to go along with Trump's plan to overturn the election . . . maybe he remembered a certain admonition from a Broadway stage performer. Maybe it was a fucking actor that saved our democracy? Imagine that!

Last year, conservatives lashed out at Bud Light after a transgender influencer promoted the brand on social media. Kid Rock was so upset, he posted a video of himself using Bud Light cans as target practice (his first hit in years!).

The right also attempted to boycott Disney over the company's opposition to that shitty "Don't Say Gay" law in Florida. But Republicans didn't really go for it. Because ~~they're all secretly bi~~ everyone loves Disney.

And remember when we (reluctantly, but willingly) stopped eating Chick-fil-A because of their donations to anti-LGBTQ causes and their President's bad comments on gay stuff?

Then they reversed course, and we all went back to dipping waffle fries in that sweet Polynesian sauce like nothing happened? All was well, until recently, when conservatives called for a (failed) boycott of Chick-fil-A because they have a VP of diversity, equity, and inclusion. (And if someone were to claim Lovett never stopped eating Chick-fil-A, just kept on downing crispy nuggs like a gay traitor without a care in the world, that would be an awful thing to suggest without proof, which you can't possibly have, right?)

Protest

This is where we separate the men from the Proud Boys. Protest is often the loudest and most visible form of organizing, and has the potential to generate the most awareness and passion around a cause. From the March on Washington to the March for Our Lives, from the Women's March to the Black Lives Matter protests, Americans have taken to the streets by the millions so that their fellow citizens would no longer be able to ignore suffering and injustice.

And hey, it's easy to get cynical about the idea of "marching for a cause" – those corny chants, the goofy signs – but when coupled with strategic, long-term organizing, protesting can be a potent force for change. It can wrest the microphone from the rich and powerful, grab people's attention, and pressure politicians to take action. And that feeling – looking around and seeing countless people marching and chanting together – that fuels the kind of inspiration required to keep a movement growing.

Keep That Insurrection in Your Pants

One last note on protesting. Yes, it would be so satisfying to see a big-ass rock go through that beautiful glass window at Starbucks. After all, you didn't drive all the way to Portland to see a garbage can just sit there undoused with kerosene. And there's just something about the way the fire looks as it burns . . . But if you really feel the need to burn this mother-fucker down – do it the responsible way: by getting arrested at a climate change demonstration with the cast of *Grace and Frankie*.

What to Do If You Find Yourself at an Insurrection

Leave?

———

Organizing is often the most harrowing step because it takes for-fucking-ever. But there is a clear path for how organizing can lead to meaningful change.

Here's a little something to put on your democracy vision board.

WHEEL OF PROGRESS

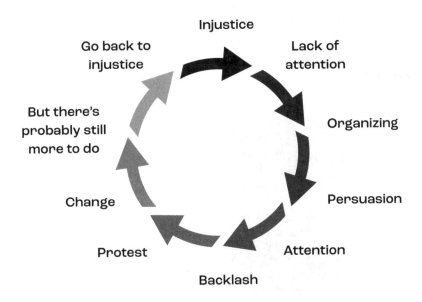

So there you have it. You're organized. You're fired up.

You've got this.

Now let's go storm the Capitol!

What Have We Learned?

- The insurrection failed because Mike Pence went to a musical
- We'll never know how many Americans merely pretended to stop eating Chick-fil-A
- When in doubt, just get some buddies together and kidnap your state's governor

Step 7

GIVE
YOURSELF
A BREAK

POP A SQUAT for a beat, kids. Elder millennials are speaking. You've made it this far, which means you've done a lot, but it doesn't feel like enough, and you're wondering if it ever will. And that means it's time . . . to do nothing.

Look, politics is a slog. It's harder than it should be. Our problems are vast. Our opponents are powerful and stupid. And sometimes, on the left, you see two ways of coping: One is to be so cynical as to believe nothing will ever change. The other is to be soooooo serious and obsessed with politics that you scold anyone who makes a joke or takes a break – that you see any kind of joy or celebration of even the smallest victories as foolish and naive. And we say fuck that.

If that's how others need to process their emotions to feel safe or superior, that's OK, that's on them. But you're not other people. You're really doing it! You've volunteered and organized and voted and persuaded and *tried*. And that means you have to find a way to pay attention and stay involved without giving up or going sour. And that means you have to take care of yourself.

Here's the thing: taking mental health breaks or even acknowledging that we're stressed or burned-out doesn't come naturally to us. In our twenties and thirties, we handled these things the old-fashioned way: by grinding our teeth and having a recurring nightmare about accidentally eating Hillary Clinton's grilled salmon, which she's desperately looking for in our childhood bedroom.

The point is, if we're being totally honest, when we first heard the term "self-care," it took us a little too long to figure out it wasn't just a euphemism for masturbation. And then we learned it can sometimes mean that too, but not all the time. And, yeah, we were prone to skepticism when internet goofs said that going "goblin mode" wasn't *just* eating chips and watching *Love Island* in dirty sweats, but also a form of political resistance.

Self-care

But we're all learning and growing and trying to be our therapists' FAVORITE. And what's also true is a culture in which generations of parents said, "Walk it off, you're fine" until bone protruded through skin was not without its own pathologies. So this step is a step to just sit with our feelings, which makes us uncomfortable, which is why it's probably good.

THINGS YOU CAN WALK OFF

CHARLEYHORSE

THINGS YOU CAN'T WALK OFF

CLIMATE CHANGE/ GENERATIONAL TRAUMA

So much of what we've been saying so far is about getting you to do more. But sometimes to do more, you have to do less. You have to put down your phone and stop scrolling. You have to spend time with friends and family and that on-again-off-again sexual partner who isn't exactly right for you but whatever. You have to give yourself enough time away from the perpetual shitstorm to have that glorious moment where the sun is shining and you breathe in deeply and exhale and realize that you didn't realize how much you needed a break. And then, when you jump back into the fight, you'll be recharged, you'll remember what politics is about in the first place, which is the life outside of it. And that spirit you bring will sustain you in the long periods of uncertainty that hang between victories.

You have to find joy in the struggle.

And that's especially true if politics is about to become your full-time job . . . And it is – in the next chapter.

What Have We Learned?

- It CAN mean masturbation, but it usually doesn't mean that
- That on-again-off-again sexual partner is NOT right for you
- Hillary's salmon was a metaphor for Lovett's imposter syndrome

Step 8

MAKE POLITICS YOUR JOB

WELCOME TO THE DIY part of democracy! This is the chapter where we explore the perks and pitfalls of a career in politics. The good news is that you won't feel as much pressure to donate to another campaign because you won't be making a lot of money. The bad news is you may have to endure such hassles as long hours, constituents yelling at you for things you can't control, and realizing that if you have to eat one more pre-made chef's salad from the Senate cafeteria you'll do an insurrection yourself. Plus, you might even get a subpoena! Up to this point, you've been a valuable part-time participant – your candidate got *Billy the Bunny Has Bi Parents* back onto the library shelf, your Women's March post went viral and got a heart from Jessica Chastain, and your speech about a NIMBY housing proposal at a city council meeting brought a hardened democratic socialist to tears. But now, you're clamoring for more. You've got a taste for making a difference, and these small plates just won't fucking do. You're thinking, "Hey – instead of spending all this time trying to elect and influence people in government, why not BECOME the government? Why tune the machine when I can *be* the machine?" And even though you're now laughing in a weird, almost evil way, it's still a great impulse, and we support you!

The time we spent working on campaigns and in government was the most exhausting period of our lives, but also the most meaningful. A job in politics can be incredibly fulfilling and – if you can avoid getting indicted or caught having sex in a hearing room – you can have a more lasting impact than the occasional volunteer shift.

So if you're interested in making democracy your full-time occupation, let's peruse the options.

Work on a Campaign

Are you a glutton for punishment who wants to re-create your college years, is capable of functioning on little to no sleep, and can survive on french fries, Diet Coke, and Diet Coke you mix with whiskey every time a new poll drops? A campaign job could be right for you! You'll discover which Hampton Inn has the best breakfast buffet (the Hampton Inn that's a Kimpton). You'll meet inspiring people and make lifelong friendships. And when the campaign ends, win or lose, it often opens the door to exciting new jobs and/or therapy topics. Maybe you'll work in government, but even if you don't, having been in that campaign kiln will have made you strong and tempered and shatter resistant no matter where your career takes you next. Working on a campaign can lead to a position in the White House and – even more impressive – a podcast. Lots of people ask us, "How can I get a job in the White House some day?" And while there are many paths – marry the president's daughter and pretend to know about the Middle East, sneak in during a state dinner, be a Portuguese water dog – one great way to get a job in the White House is to move as far from Washington as you can and get a job on a campaign somewhere, anywhere.

Campaigns come in all different shapes and sizes – at all different levels of government.

Presidential

The most high-profile campaign you can work on, but they only come around every four years. If you work for a candidate during the presidential primary, it's kind of like getting in on the ground floor of a start-up (with the same chance that it will crash and burn). Working on a presidential campaign is all-consuming. The job becomes your life. Which can be exciting – the stakes are high, the work is endless, and so are the opportunities to contribute and prove yourself. But it's also likely to mean that you are a terrible spouse/partner/relative/friend for a while, and that can leave a mark. Winning is thrilling and opens up a world of possibility in Washington, DC. Losing to another Democrat in the primary is tough, but if you're willing to suck it up and swallow your pride, you're still well positioned to get a job working for the eventual nominee in the general election. Losing a general election is devastating.

But even losing campaigns can teach you a lot, and we know that because each of us has been there.

Statewide (Governor, Senate)

A great way to gain experience on a big-budget campaign with a seasoned incumbent or a rising star in your state. Winning one of these races is a huge deal. Your boss could be one of only 100 senators or a governor who has the power to do an enormous amount of good for their state. You'll also get to work with professionals you can learn from, and since it's smaller than a presidential campaign you'll have real responsibilities, which means more opportunities to advance and pick up new skills if you don't blow it.

House Races

You get to hobnob with an eclectic mix of candidates, many of whom have little to no political experience and may in fact be just some random person, like you! But the stakes are still high, you can play an important role in flipping or holding a crucial seat, and if you do a good job, you could get a pretty sweet gig in your candidate's congressional office (or at least a gig that's a step above the interns).

Local (Mayor, City Council, School Board)

Again, the smallest races often have the most influence. The lower the budget, the fewer the staff, and the more chances for you to learn by taking on more responsibilities. You never know what the future holds for that district attorney you help to get elected – she could become the first female vice president or the latest governor of Illinois to go to jail. But hey, you can't win if you don't play! Local politicians often have the power to make the most tangible, lasting impact on the lives of the people they represent.

———

Once you've chosen the type of campaign you want to work for, you need to consider which positions are best suited to your capabilities.

Communications

The communications team shapes the campaign's message and figures out the best way to convey that message to voters through the candidate's speeches and events, through social and digital media, and to reporters. Roles include dealing with reporters as a press staffer, speech writing, event planning, digital strategy, and rapid response. This is where the three of us got our starts. It was a long time ago. It was did-you-get-my-fax years ago. It was wow-this-phone-has-email years ago.

Field

Field staffers organize the campaign's volunteers, build crowds for events, and help register, talk to, and turn out voters on Election Day. See the country! Sleep on couches! Make all the difference by being one of the people who actually persuades real voters without getting imprisoned in any of their sex dungeons.

Fundraising

Do you like begging rich people for money and/or coming up with creative new ways for your boss to beg rich people for money? Finally, this is your chance to be on the other side of those annoying emails and texts you get from campaigns (AND get unsolicited advice about how to reach working-class voters from people who haven't flown commercial since the '80s!). These are the staffers who raise the (sometimes ungodly) sums of money that are necessary to fund the campaign. So they are very important and also very good at dignified groveling.

Policy

The policy team works with the candidate to form positions and proposals or, in some cases, to take what a candidate has already been saying for months and turn it into a policy that makes sense. This is a great position for people who have multiple postgraduate degrees and the debt to prove it. (Note: If you're relatively young and new to politics, don't be the person who says, "I want to work in policy" and acts like field jobs are beneath you. They are not, and your youthful confidence offends hardened campaign operatives who have been broken by primary defeats from before you were born.)

Research

The group that digs into the candidate's voting history and past statements, as well as their opponent's record. It's a perfect job for anyone who can type at a desk for 12 hours without getting up to pee. Be the person who unearths the sex scandal that takes down your opponent and hopefully not the candidate you're working for! (But hey, that's a fun story too.) Research can be the difference between winning an election and losing to someone who made up his life story and has an open warrant in Brazil.

Other Roles

These include scheduling, advance, campaign management, operations, personal assistant, videographer/sex partner (looking at you, John Edwards), bus driver, Diet Coke valet, stylist, Dominion Voting Systems "technician," pollster, ad maker, consultant who gets paid handsomely to give obvious advice, consultant who gets paid handsomely to give bad advice, candidate's friend who tells said consultant to just "let the candidate be the candidate," and drug mule.

Grab a Hoof, Boys

In 2004, I worked on the John Edwards for President campaign. (Again, it was before all the bad stuff.) I was the communications director's assistant, which meant lots of administrative work (that I was *terrible* at) and fetching of meals (this part I nailed, especially when he was on the Atkins diet and I had to remember to remove all the buns from burger-like items). For the last few months of the campaign, Edwards sent me to Iowa and then New Hampshire to drive the traveling press corps around and fetch them food (they were a pro-bun crew). One freezing-cold January night, another volunteer named Charlie and I were dispatched to pick up the traveling press corps at an airport that was so far north that it wasn't even on our map of New Hampshire. It was snowing and windy, and the visibility was terrible. I remember seeing two massive figures looming in the distance. By the time I figured out what they were, they were basically on top of us, and all I could think to do was scream, "MOOOOOSE!" (Helpful!) Miraculously, we swerved just enough to miss the big one and instead hit his smaller friend. After thanking God we were still alive, we called the cops. When the state trooper finally arrived, we asked, "How are you going to get this thing out of the middle of the road?" To which he replied, "Grab a hoof, boys!" Like we said, no job is too small.

Sell Yourself Short

In 2004, I worked on the John Kerry for President campaign. (He beat Tommy's candidate and did so without a mistress . . . that we know of.) I started out as the sole assistant to the entire communications team, which meant I had a lot of lunches to get and calls to transfer. I also had to wake up at 4 am every day, read all the news I could find, and copy/paste the most relevant stories into a document that was then emailed to the staff and often faxed to the candidate himself. I happened to sit next to the campaign's head speechwriter, and when a position opened for a deputy speechwriter, I asked him if I could have the job. He immediately said no, probably because I had absolutely no experience as a speechwriter. A few weeks later, he still hadn't filled the job, mostly because no one wanted to work on a campaign that was losing badly to Howard Dean (google the "I Have a Scream" speech). The campaign was also so broke that they couldn't pay the going rate for a speechwriter. As someone who was already working on this broke, losing campaign for a salary of $24,000 per year, I became the most (only) affordable option and finally got the job.

Work in Government

Maybe the rough-and-tumble of campaign life isn't for you. Are you looking for a stable job with benefits, overtime, and relentless bureaucracy, punctuated by transcendent moments in which real change is still somehow possible? Then the public sector is where you belong! There are many jobs at many levels of government, so let's take a look at the many wonderful places you can work if you pass a drug test.

White House

A job in the White House is an incredible, once-in-a-lifetime opportunity to work directly for the most powerful person on the planet. Even if the administration's legislative agenda is ground to a halt by a bunch of yahoos in Congress, the

President still gets to do a lot, like conducting foreign policy or issuing executive orders. White House jobs are grueling, but fast-paced and exciting. You will meet lots of brilliant, well-meaning people (and some real dipshits) and be a part of history. A quick note for those who dream of one day recreating a scene from *The West Wing* . . . Very few people actually get to work in the White House. The West Wing and parts of the East Wing have space for staff, but much of the building is used as a residence or museum or document-flushing center. Most administration staffers work in neighboring office buildings, like the (thrillingly named) Eisenhower Executive Office Building. That's where we stuck Lovett.

They Shouldn't Have Let Me Give Tours

There was this wonderful era in which a lot of Democratic politicians pretended to have some nonsensical objection to gay marriage but were for civil unions, which was marriage in all but name. And believe it or not, this was enough to get applause for a while because Republicans were so seethingly homophobic (and amending state constitutions to ban marriage equality) that Democrats looked good by comparison. Classic us. Anyway, during this time, I was a speechwriter. My friends Steve and Justin asked me to perform their wedding ceremony because they wanted someone who ~~would not take too much~~

~~attention~~ loved them. But because the reception was in West Virginia, a state where gay marriage was illegal at the time, the marriage certificate would have to be issued and signed in DC. And then we realized: I could get certified to perform legal, official weddings in the District of Columbia, *and* I could give White House tours. So that's what happened. One night, Steve, Justin, and I wandered into the Rose Garden. I asked the questions and they said "I do" and did a tour-appropriate kiss. And it was done! Gay rights! The certificate even lists the ceremony's official location as 1600 Pennsylvania Avenue. It's now a decade later, and Justin and Steve ~~were at the insurrection~~ are still happily married, the first gay couple to be legally wed at the White House.

———

Capitol Hill

Work for a senator or representative in a legislative, press, or constituent services role. What are constituent services? Basically, customer service for the people who live in your district or state. Pro: help people with a problem that only government intervention can solve. Con: if you mess up, angry constituents will Yelp the living crap out of you! Working on the Hill places you at the epicenter of every big legislative story and allows you to make friendships that could last from two to six years.

Abdul El-Sayed

Physician, professor, epidemiologist, author, host of the Crooked Media podcast *America Dissected*, former health director of Detroit, current director of the Health, Human, and Veterans Services Department in Wayne County.

Why work in local government?

When you attempt to wrap your mind around the complexity that is federal policy and politics, that can get a little too big to fully appreciate. Every day I go to work and my job is to think about the health and well-being of 1.8 million people who live in a very particular place that I can name. I can drive to them, and I can knock on their doors, and I can ask them, "What would you like your local health and human services department to be working on?" And I can have a conversation with them. I can see them when they step into our clinics, or they come get our services, or they come to our events. That everyday gives me a sense of both fulfillment and a sense of joy at what public service is supposed to be about.

I also love the fact that when they disagree with me, they know who I am, they know where I sit, and they can share that disagreement. You can think back to the founding fathers and ask what their experience was with the government they envisioned, in contrast to what they were fighting against in terms of tyranny and a government that was very far away. And I believe they envisioned something like what local government is today.

Government Agencies

There are over a million jobs at various cabinet agencies, like State, Education, Labor, Veterans Affairs, etc. Some are political appointees chosen by each new administration. There are also career gigs where you are there to implement that department's mission from the ground up – no matter who won the last election. For example, when Congress passes a major climate bill, it's the administration of that law, at places like the Environmental Protection Agency or the Department of the Treasury, that actually determines whether the law's promises are kept – whether emissions get reduced and cows get replaced by 3D-printed lab meat or whatever. Our government only works as well as the people who choose to make public service a profession and view it as a calling. Plus, when you retire, you'll be given a party with all the joy of an episode of *Severance*.

Deep State

The Deep State is made up of government agencies like the Department of Defense, the CIA, the Department of Justice, and other corrupt wings of the Democratic establishment – a satanic cabal that rigs elections, plants pee tapes, controls the weather, and fluoridates the water to weaken our collective resolve.

———

Washington can be a fun place to live and work – we were there from the first BlackBerry to the fifth iPhone. There are so many neat things to see and do.

Air and Jewish Space Laser Museum

Washington Monument, The Nation's Penis

MUSEUMS!

MONUMENTS!

DC AMERICA'S SWAMP

The Watergate Hotel

The Mayflower Hotel

SCANDALS!

THE MANY STORIED HOTELS WHERE POLITICIANS HAVE BROUGHT PROSTITUTES

Of course, you don't have to go to Washington to work for the government. There are millions of public sector jobs all across the country, including federal prosecutors, TSA agents, National Park Service rangers, CDC employees, and about 87,000 new IRS agents.

Other Political Jobs

Nonprofit/NGO

Do you like having meetings about having meetings? Well, then a nonprofit or nongovernmental organization could be just the place for you. This is your chance to make a difference from the outside. At best, you will have the opportunity to directly work on an issue you care about without getting bogged down by the complicated rules and procedures of government. At worst, the power gets turned off because you're a bunch of social justice activists who studied comparative literature and no one knows how to use QuickBooks.

Public Advocacy Organization

Every day, in DC and state capitals across the country, there are people who wake up and think, "In the game of government, it's time to work the shit out of these refs." Corporations will spend millions on ad campaigns and lobbying efforts to "educate" and pressure legislators and government agencies – it could be to stop environmental regulations, protect their monopoly on an industry, avoid taxes, or keep chickens miserable. Public advocacy groups are there, often with far fewer resources, to fight against corporate interests for policies that lower carbon emissions, create safer workplaces, and reduce prescription costs. How? Through lobbying, research, and throwing soup on the Mona Lisa.

Think Tank

These are institutions, some of which are "prestigious" and have been around forever, that use donations from wealthy backers (and in some cases Middle Eastern autocrats) to fund research, policy work, polling, and jobs for former high-ranking government officials to do some well-heeled "spitballing" and "steak eating." There are also right-wing think tanks which exist to pump out policy papers that tell us why the minimum wage actually sucks and birds love oil pipelines if you ever bothered to ask one. But many think tanks have nonpartisan public service missions and fund important projects that help us understand everything from economic inequality to abortion access. You can help them churn out new ideas and build support for those ideas by working to persuade politicians and the public.

Political Consulting

Campaigns and organizations often hire outside firms to help them figure out how to tell their story, understand what voters are thinking, advertise, or get better press coverage. Ideally this happens before a scandal, but sometimes, it's after. Like an episode of *Black Mirror*, some consultants can change how you think about an issue forever; others can fill an hour, say nothing, and leave you wondering why you even bothered. Consulting is sort of what you make of it. (We did some consulting work back in the day, and we're mostly sure we're not mostly evil, for example.) There are lots of cool opportunities fresh out of college to work with progressive firms that do polling, ad making, PR, digital media, political strategy, etc. At best, you'll get to learn about a bunch of different campaigns and companies and work for smart people who spend all day thinking about messaging and storytelling. At worst, you end up collecting souls for Kellyanne Conway.

Internships

A good way to learn and potentially find yourself at the center of a high-profile impeachment proceeding. There's a decent chance that your day-to-day responsibilities will involve answering phones, picking up or sorting mail, and constantly being a little afraid that if you mess up this one small task everyone will know it was you (and they will). But you will also learn a lot and start relationships that can be helpful down the road.

Obama's Favorite

Make no mistake, working in politics is a grind. It can be tedious, thankless, and threaten your sanity. But it is also filled with a million little victories along the way. There are early mornings putting yard signs up after they were ripped down the night before. But there are also days when your candidate wins, and some MAGA drone has to go back to working for his father-in-law. You will put in more hours than you ever imagined, and give more of yourself than you ever knew you had. And then, at your most burned-out, you unexpectedly find yourself on the Truman Balcony of the White House toasting the fact that tens of millions of people can now get health care because of the Affordable Care Act you helped get passed. And that's when President Obama pulls you aside and whispers softly in your ear, "You were always my favorite staffer, Ben Rhodes." Suddenly, it will all seem worthwhile – until you wake up the next day and have to start that process all over again.

What Have We Learned?

- Every interest is special
- Tommy ran over a fucking moose
- Obama loves Ben Rhodes the most

Step 9

THE MOST IMPORTANT ELECTION OF OUR LIFETIME (YOURS!)

YOU'RE FINALLY READY to take the ultimate leap. You've seen how the sausage is made, and now you want to . . . be the sausage? Maybe you sense a higher calling, or maybe you want to get elected so that you can pardon yourself for all those pesky felonies. Whatever the reason, you've decided to throw your hat in the three-ring circus of running for office. You've already put yourself through hell to save democracy – why not put everyone else in your life through hell too? Running for office requires all the skills you've developed on your journey thus far. You will engage with voters, donors, and volunteers. You will have to know history unless you're running in Florida. You will be forced to raise money, organize, navigate what's left of the media, and read about what your freshman college roommate really thought of you. And remember how you spent hours trying to get folks to turn out for your candidate? You're gonna have to convince them to show up at the polls – but this time, it's for you. Fear not. If you've read this far, you have as much political experience as many of our elected officials.

Launching a campaign is a massive undertaking and a big gamble. You may lose. Or, even more terrifying, you might win. You might get the best chance you'll ever have to actually make decisions that can help the people you've been wanting to help since you first cast that ballot back in Step 3. Either way, you'll be exposing yourself in a way you never have before. (Hopefully, you've never exposed yourself before because that will for sure come out during the campaign.)

So now we're gonna walk you through what it takes to make a run for it. Before you file the paperwork to seek office and do an awkward photo shoot with your family that screams, "I'm totally normal, and even if I've tried drugs I'm not a big drug person," there are several items on the "to-do before running" list. We've broken down the entire process, from the decision to take the plunge through election night, into a simple 17-point plan. Starting with that ever-so-essential question . . .

1. Why do you want to run?

For God? For country? For a congressional gym membership? You will be asked this question many times over the next 18 to 24 months, so you need to figure it out. If you don't have any idea why you're running for office, you probably shouldn't be running for office. If you're running to fill a gaping chasm in your soul, it won't work, but I guess we can't stop you. Regardless, there are a few things you can do before running that will help you nail the answer. For starters, go talk to the people you want to represent. You will be doing a lot of speaking on the campaign trail, so for now try to shut the fuck up. Attend community gatherings and city council meetings. Meet with as many people as you can, and actually listen to what they have to say. Find out their hopes, their challenges, what they want you to do for them if elected. It will help focus your campaign.

2. Determine which office is right for you

Do you wanna be a big fish in a small pond or a small fish in a fetid swamp? Consider where you think your talents will be the most useful. Make sure you have a connection to the district or state you're running in. Also, make sure you actually live in the district or state you're running in. For example, let's say you're a TV doctor who wants to be the next senator from Pennsylvania – it's probably not ideal for your primary residence to be in New Jersey (or for nine of your ten properties to not be in Pennsylvania, or for you to tweet about how you own ten properties).

3. Vet yourself before you wreck yourself

Are you qualified? Doesn't matter! Do you lack charisma? So does the Senate. But you need to know your strengths and (especially) your weaknesses. As a candidate, every detail of your past and present will be combed over like Joe Biden's hair plugs. The news is a business, and now they're gonna make *your* business *their* business. So you want to get out in front of any old Facebook posts or ongoing financial crimes that might preclude a run for public office.

CHAPPAQUIDD-O-METER

DIRT: You went to a Halloween party in college, and there is video of you . . . in blackface, doing a bit from an old Chris Rock special.

RATING: 5 Chappaquiddicks

DIRT: You once strapped your dog to the roof of your station wagon during a family road trip.

RATING: 3 Chappaquiddicks

DIRT: You dodged the draft.

RATING: 1.5 Chappaquiddicks

DIRT: You call your wife "Mother."
RATING: No Chappaquiddicks, but somehow worse.

The most important vetting process is the one you do of yourself (this also doesn't mean masturbation). You have to understand that past votes (or not voting), business deals, investments, social media posts, or alleged membership in a Soviet Bloc nationalist organization with Nazi ties are all considered fair game in politics. Now if you're running for state assembly, you may not face that much scrutiny, but if you are running for Congress or any statewide position, you will have researchers poring over your life. If there are unsavory personal details you don't mind the whole world knowing, you should be OK – shamelessness is a real political asset these days! But even if you're a veritable Girl Scout with no digital footprint, operatives can misrepresent and slime you, and that sucks. But also remember that Donald Trump was elected president, so run like nobody's watching.

4. Craft a narrative

Politics is all about marketing! Maybe you came from nothing. That's great. Maybe you went to a college that had buildings with your name on them. Less great. But we can still work with that. Point is, if you want to get elected, you need to juice the shit out of your life for the details that make you seem the most relatable. Crafting a strong narrative is essential to your success as a candidate. And if you don't have a strong narrative, you can always just make one up and hope nobody ever finds out you're not really Jewish, your grandparents didn't survive the Holocaust, your mom was not in the South Tower during 9/11, you lied about where you went to high school and college, you never worked a day at Goldman Sachs, you used a veteran's dying dog to set up a bogus fundraiser, and you stole puppies from the Amish (allegedly!).

Danica Roem

Journalist turned State Senator (VA-30), the first openly trans person ever elected to a US state legislature, and executive director of *Emerge Virginia*.

Can research really make a difference in your campaign?

Do not undervalue research. My God! This is one thing that Democrats very often get wrong, and that we have to consider as a mandatory part of a campaign. So often, research books – on yourself and on the person or people running against you – are seen as something only done in top-tier or high-budgeted races. Opposition research needs to be seen as essential as hiring a campaign manager or sending out direct mail. If you are a Democrat and your name is on the ballot, your local, state, or national party needs to say, "OK, here's the book on yourself, and here's the book on the other people." That is so important. You need to know who you are on the internet, and beyond that, you need to know what image of you is out there, and you need to know what the image of the other person is.

And hey, we weren't all born with a silver sob story in our mouth. If your great-grandfather was a steel tycoon, you could say something like, "My great-grandpa Bud used to wake up every morning and go to work at a steel mill." Yes, technically, he owned the mill. But he did keep an office (and gay paramour) there.

Now it's possible you may have trouble talking so much about yourself – and if that's the case, get the fuck out of this chapter, you well-adjusted freak. Running for office is not for you.

5. Come up with a winning slogan

Every campaign needs a catchy slogan. And there are many ways to go about finding one. Some of the most iconic lines have involved wordplay with a candidate's name. For example, "Keep Cool With Coolidge," or "Grant Us Another Term," or "They Can't Lick Our Dick" (which an intensive Google search suggests was actually used on Nixon campaign merch). You can also go for something more timeless like Obama's "Change We Can Believe In" or Reagan's "Let's Make America Great Again" – which proved to be so timeless, it was recycled in 2016. But don't be afraid to take a big swing. Like these slogans, one of which is real. Can you guess which one?

It's the anti-Prohibition line on the right – from Al Smith's failed 1928 campaign. Smith got crushed by Herbert Hoover. (Hoover and the Republicans promised "a chicken in every pot and a car in every garage." A year later, when people looked in their pots for that chicken, they found the Great Depression.)

6. Build a team

Find people who will advise you, work on your campaign, endorse you, and hopefully not write a disparaging tell-all book about you later. You will need people who understand the district or state you're running in, have great contacts, know the issues, and – most of all – who will tell you the truth. Whoever told Ron DeSantis he had a winning smile and looked normal in those lifts did that man a real disservice! You will also need lots and lots of volunteers and luck.

7. Announce you're announcing

You're getting closer to the big day, but you still have a very important item left. Before you can make your official announcement, you might be able to get some extra press coverage by announcing that you are making an announcement. By announcing you're announcing you will give voters a crucial 12-hour window to google who you are.

8. Announce you're running

There are many approaches here – a major speech in front of thousands of supporters, a live interview on Twitter Spaces that's riddled with glitches, descending a golden escalator to declare the American dream dead. This is a chance for you to start defining your campaign (so don't fuck it up!). The most important questions for you to answer here are "Why me?" "Why now?" and "Did I successfully cover up that hit-and-run?"

9–15. Raise some money

Remember Step 4? On donating? And how much our broken system depends on fundraising through endless texts and emails? Well, now you're gonna be sending "please help me, the quarter is ending and my campaign is on life support" texts like it's your job. (Because it is! Or at least, it's the job of someone you hired.) You're gonna be on the phone around the clock, leaving voicemails like an overbearing parent during spring break, trying to get every old friend, casual acquaintance, and D-list celebrity you know to drop some cash and/or post a donation link.

16. Hit the campaign trail

Now you're in it. You're doing rallies, town halls, debates, shaking hands, eating meats on sticks, proving you know how to hold a beer, proving you know how to hold a baby, proving you know how to hold a hot dog, etc. The campaign trail is where you will put all that listening you did to good use, try to win over voters with policies that prove you understand their problems and promises that are at least theoretically achievable, even if they won't be easy to fulfill. There's a reason every kid running for student council promises pizza on Fridays. Because it fucking works. So what's your pizza on Fridays?

Also be sure to find moments that showcase your lighter side. (Note: If you don't have a sense of humor, that is not an insurmountable problem – some of our most successful politicians are absolutely humorless.) Every appearance can benefit from a couple of well-placed zingers. You want to come across as naturally fun without trying too hard to be funny (you're Amy Klobuchar, not Amy Sedaris).

Jokes Are Hard

Jokes are high risk/high reward. If a joke in a speech lands, everybody's laughing and having a great time and thinking, "This politician gets me. Where do I donate?" But when a joke bombs, it sucks the life out of a room. One time, President Obama had to speak at a fundraiser organized by Whoopi Goldberg at a showing of *Sister Act* on Broadway. He was going to speak onstage after the musical, and because that's a weird thing for the president of the United States to do, he asked for a joke to use at the top. I thought for a second, had nothing, and said – and please note that I hate typing this, hate that I said this, still want to die thinking about this – "Uh, I hope you enjoyed *Sister Act*, now here's my brother act?" His face issued a little grimace, and he said, simply, "No."

I immediately sweated through my suit – just completely. Then President Obama looked at his watch and said that I had half an hour to beat whatever that was. Now I'm in a full panic. And right before he goes out, he sees me and says with a smirk, "Got anything?"

Here's what I had: "What a great event. First of all, I've always loved *Sister Act*. Second, it's helpful with my research on convents to send Sasha and Malia after high school."

He laughed (a joke in the dad sweet spot), gave me a fist bump, and a look that wasn't approval so much as tacit permission to continue to exist.

———

17. Win/lose/concede/file lawsuit

On Election Day (or a few days after depending on the mail-in ballot situation), you will find out the results. Once the race has been called by reputable sources and is outside the margin for a mandatory recount – you can either declare victory, graciously concede, or file as many frivolous lawsuits as possible.

And if you lose, don't fret – you can always try again! Lots of candidates who lost elections later went on to win: Obama, Reagan, Nixon, Hitler. Joe Biden ran for president three times before he won (2008, 1988, 1824).

Hillary Clinton

What went wrong in 2016

In a way, it was a lack of imagination about what could happen. We should have understood that the media loved it. The more outrageous you are, the better the ratings are, and we did not compete at all in that arena, and so, you know, I should have thrown some more insults or advocated some more crazy stuff. I should have just made a long list and gotten smart people, called you guys, said, "OK, give me the weirdest things you think could happen and let's be prepared for it."

We Were Such Losers in ~~High School~~ 2004

When I worked for the John Edwards campaign in 2004, we had a small but scrappy team of young, dedicated, fun people. John was inexperienced but had a ton of political talent, an inspiring story, and the ability to connect with voters. And despite the fact that we lost, we kinda won? Edwards went from first-term senator to the Democratic nominee for vice president! Of course, we didn't know that at the time (Edwards wasn't selected to be Kerry's pick for vice president until months after he dropped out), but we knew that we had outperformed expectations and outlasted politicians with more money and better name ID. So on the night we officially lost, we partied, celebrated our accomplishments, and felt proud. Coulda been a lot worse. (And it was for anyone who worked on his 2008 campaign!)

After John Kerry lost the 2004 campaign, I was crushed. I couldn't imagine four more years of George W. Bush, I felt like we let down half the country, and I had no idea what I was going to do with my life. I packed up my tiny basement apartment in DC and drove home to Massachusetts so I could move back in with my parents because I was broke – so broke that I blew through the last toll on the Mass Pike without paying. And just when I thought I was done with politics and would finally make my parents happy by applying to law school, I got a message from my old boss, Robert Gibbs: "Barack Obama is looking for a speechwriter."

———

Amanda Litman

Co-founder and co-executive director of *Run For Something*, an organization that recruits young, diverse progressives to run for office.

Why you should "run for something"

After the 2016 election, I was looking around for someone to solve the problem of how to get good people into office. I was looking for the grown-ups in the room, because surely somebody must have created an organization that would do this. This is not an innovative idea. Get more people to run for office. It's not groundbreaking!

I quickly realized there were no grown-ups. If I wanted a place for my peers, my friends, and the people asking me for help to get involved, I had to create it myself. I had to open the door for new leaders and then help them walk through it – that's the story of *Run for Something*.

Since our work began, we've seen that when you get good people into government, the government can do really good things. It can change housing laws. It can change school curriculums. It can make it easier and more accessible for people to vote and participate in the democratic process. It can protect and expand abortion access. We have seen over and over again that if normal people – totally extraordinary, but also totally ordinary people – actually engage as leaders, they pass legislation that makes life better for us all.

Here's the secret: Nobody's born a politician. The way you become a politician is the same way you become an artist, or a musician, or a writer, or a carpenter.

You do it. You put your name on the ballot, and you start talking to people about the things that you care about, and you hear what they care about. You can, and absolutely should, get into this even if you don't think you were made for it. People stupider than you are doing it, people who care less than you are doing it, people who aren't as committed to the issues that you give a shit about are doing it. Malicious actors are doing it. The only qualifications that you need – beyond the legal ones, like residency, age, and whatever else is required by the office you want to run for – is that you need to be willing to work and willing to listen. Everything else you can learn.

Anyone Can Get Elected

You may feel that running for office is out of your grasp, that you don't deserve such an exalted position in the public sphere. And whenever you feel that way, just consider these two words: Matt Gaetz. There is no surefire path or prerequisite to get elected, but many politicians had regular jobs earlier in their careers that no doubt shaped their politics. Long before she became the first member of Congress to get ejected from *Beetlejuice: The Musical*, Lauren Boebert owned a gun-themed restaurant that was accused of giving dozens of people explosive diarrhea at a rodeo. Barack Obama worked at Baskin-Robbins back when he was growing up ~~in Kenya~~ in America. As a summer lifeguard in Illinois, Ronald Reagan is said to have rescued 77 people from drowning, which would either make Rock River one of the most treacherous bodies of water on Earth or this is a bit of an exaggeration. Jim Jordan was an assistant wrestling coach at Ohio State, and by all accounts that went super well. Politicians come from all different backgrounds – you never know how your personal experience will help you down the line.

★ ASK SOMEONE SMARTER THAN US ★

Danica Roem

On the importance of training

My job is to train, recruit, and train Democratic women to run for office. It's the single most important thing you can do. And I don't say that because they're paying me as executive director [of *Emerge Virginia*]. I went through that training before I did this and I won. I unseated the self-described "chief homophobe" of Virginia. In the training that you do, you will explore your insecurities, your vulnerabilities, your questions. Most importantly, you're going to explore all of those things with a group of people who have the same fears that you do, and you realize you don't need to have imposter syndrome.

But the thing I stress all the time is that you don't have to have the most money to win, although it is very nice to have that, and it's certainly helpful. You need to have enough money to execute your game plan. That is the thing that is never talked about in politics: Have a game plan, stick to the plan, make adjustments on a tactical basis as opposed to a strategic basis.

Become President

Once you've run/won/lost/gotten some name recognition/ hosted a reality show/been born a Bush or Kennedy, you may suddenly find yourself president of the United States. If this happens to you, do not panic. The country mostly runs itself. Plus, even though the job is so stressful and impossible that we literally watch presidents age right before our eyes like that Nazi who drank from the wrong cup in *Indiana Jones*, there are so many awesome perks. Think about how much more productive you'd be in your job if you had a bowling alley in your basement *and* three helicopters. Sure, you get blamed for every problem and take countless meetings where someone shows you a grainy aerial photo of a shipping yard and explains why something being built there could kill us all, but also you get to meet your favorite athletes!

This is your chance to save democracy – by spending four to eight years in charge of it, unless you die in office, which happens almost 20 percent of the time. (Or, glass half full, there's a more than 80 percent chance you'll survive.) Anyway, let's focus on making the most of whatever time you have left.

After all, you are now the leader of the free-ish world. But you're pulled in a hundred different directions and constantly responding to events out of your control. Do you think Barack Obama ran for president hoping to one day plug a massive oil spill in the Gulf of Mexico? No. But the Deepwater Horizon disaster consumed his presidency for months. Do you think Jimmy Carter was planning to be personally attacked by a swamp rabbit while he was president, an event that really took place? Of course not. But hey, you're the one who wanted to be president, so suck it up, appoint some judges, keep us out of war, do as many executive orders as your lawyers will allow, and throw a couple of medals around Tom Hanks's neck while you have the goddamn chance. After all, within months (weeks? hours?) of taking office, the honeymoon will be over and you'll likely be mired in crisis or scandal. So make hay while the sun shines. And for the love of God, don't forget to pick up your son's laptop at that repair place in Delaware.

The Presidency Is a Weird Job

One of the most fun and stressful parts of being a presidential speechwriter is getting to work on the president's speech for the White House Correspondents' Dinner, something Jon and I did together many times. This is an annual roast/ritual in which journalists, celebrities, and politicians gather at a gala at which the president of the United States is meant to do a literal comedy routine. In the days leading up to the speech in 2011, after collecting hundreds of jokes from comedy writers and speechwriters who graciously pitched in, and after a week in which the president's actual birth certificate from Hawaii was revealed, which required us to rewrite a ton of "Where's the birth certificate, Obama?" material, we were ready to show the president a draft. But there was one problem. We couldn't get any time in the Oval Office. There had been a storm in the

Midwest and a delayed rocket launch at NASA, and President Obama's attention was needed in the Situation Room. The nerve! The speech is *tomorrow* and this is important!

Finally, it's the day of the event and we met with the president. We went through the draft. Thankfully, he liked it, laughed as he read, and only tweaked one line.

There had been a joke that referenced Osama bin Laden. He asked us to change it, requesting a more current reference. So we did that. We also included a few bangers making fun of Donald Trump because the *Apprentice* host (who had been spreading a conspiracy theory that President Obama wasn't born in the US) was in attendance that year. The appointed hour arrives. The president's tight 15 crushes. In fact, the jokes mocking Trump were so withering and perfect we never heard his name again.

This was Saturday night. The next day, we found out why President Obama's schedule was so jammed, and why the joke brigade had to wait so long for our chance to discuss our little yucks. That was the weekend the president had ordered the raid on bin Laden's compound in Pakistan. That was what was on his mind while he was nonchalantly tossing a football and asking us to make one tweak.

The Presidency Is Not a
Popularity Contest

At the 2012 Democratic National Convention, Obama gave an acceptance speech that was later panned by a few pundits. We had all been really happy with the final product and the reaction from the crowd, so the media critiques naturally pissed us off. I remember complaining with the president about a particularly snarky *Politico* story during our flight home the next day, which was therapeutic for both of us. But then I went on just a little too long until he finally stopped me and said, "Hey man, how do you think I feel? Every day, I wake up knowing that at least half the country doesn't like me and thinks I'm bad at my job."

Fair point! But he wasn't done: "If I spent all my time worrying about what people think of me, I'd never get anything done. All I can do is get the best information, listen to the smartest people, ask the right questions, look for differing opinions, and then make a decision. After that, I have to just let the chips fall where they may, knowing that some people might like my decision, and some people might not. But I can't let the criticism get me down or paralyze me because I have to move on to the next decision. That's what I've learned about being president, and that's the job I signed up for."

———

THE CIRCLE OF POLITICAL LIFE

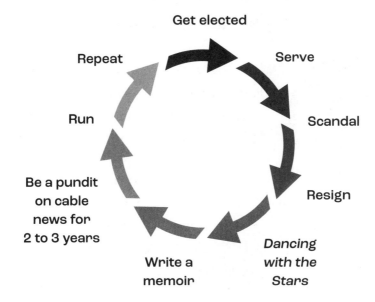

So that's that. Maybe you were impeached or maybe you threw up on the Prime Minister of Japan. But you'll be back. The only thing Americans love more than watching someone's career slowly bleed out is resurrecting it from the dead. Ellen goes to football games with George W. Bush. Life is long!

What Have We Learned?

- Promises made don't always have to be kept
- The White House has a bowling alley in the basement
- Our dumb jokes caused Trump

Step 10

A RACE
WITH NO
FINISH LINE

YOU MADE IT! You got informed, you voted, you gave your money and your time, you organized and marched, and you rose through the ranks of public servants to become a disgraced one-term president of the United States.

And yet... problems remain. In fact, while you were working on some old problems, whole new problems emerged. "Sorry, I was attending to the glaciers. When did Elon Musk gain control of Ukraine's internet?"

The work of democracy is never over. And that's a feature, not a bug. For centuries, there was nothing in the world like this. People organized themselves through power and violence. And then one day, people decided to take a chance on each other – on a government by the many, not the few, organized by laws, not kings.

Turns out, that's a tough thing to pull off. At best, democracy is messy, contentious, and infuriating. Change will be slow because convincing a big group of people to do anything is slow. Have you ever watched a table for 12 try to order at a restaurant? It's a nightmare.

But here's the amazing part. Democracy isn't just how we organize our government. It's a way to see ourselves. In deciding that we are in charge – that we have agency – we are also deciding that each of us matters and deserves a voice, that all of us are worthy of dignity and respect. In empowering us, democracy changes us.

And the reason we're all still here, grinding and vibing, is because of all the people who kept this democracy safe and made it stronger. They expanded it to include voices that were purposefully excluded. They defended it from every kind of mob and would-be tyrant. And none of those defenders were inherently better than you. They didn't even have computers. They didn't figure out that you could bring liquid soap into the shower until like, what, the 1990s? Fuckin' idiots.

The truth is, democracy is a race with no finish line. And yes, we know that sounds like running as fast and as hard as you can forever. Sorry. But if we started this book by telling you that, you wouldn't have made it this far. We had to hook you in with a good story and the promise of quick returns. Plus, we did lots of fun illustrations. And we had some laughs, didn't we? We did. We sure did.

But now you've made it to the end. And you know what it takes. You know how much work there is to do. Will it always feel like fascism is nipping at our heels? Will the stakes always feel so total? Hopefully not, but the impulse to rule by fear and force isn't going anywhere – it's as old as civilization. Donald Trump is hardly the first demagogue to pit people against each other, and he won't be the last.

The three of us remember how dark it felt at the end of 2016. We had just spent years of our lives on campaigns and in government trying to make whatever progress we could, even if it wasn't nearly enough. Now all that was at risk, and so much more. We had started a podcast earlier that year as a hobby to work through our anxieties about the election, which morphed into unfounded optimism about the outcome, when it turned out that optimism wasn't what we needed.

What we needed is what everyone did next. Protestors piling into airports. Marchers filling the streets. Activists refusing to leave congressional offices, determined to be heard. People who had barely followed the news were suddenly organizing their entire districts. People who had never cared about politics were figuring out how to run for office. People who didn't know each other or always agree with each other decided to take a chance on each other and trust each other. People we've been lucky to meet over the last eight years, as we've traveled across the country.

Before the midterm elections in 2018, we did a live show in Denver that we ended by taking a few questions from the audience. The last one came from a young woman who told us that she had driven all the way there from Utah. She was a Dreamer – an undocumented immigrant who came to America as a child – and as she started speaking, her voice began to crack: "I've lived here for a very long time, and this is the first time I've ever been scared of not being a citizen."

It took about two seconds for someone in the crowd to shout, "We love you." And suddenly a few thousand people were on their feet clapping and cheering and wiping away tears. The young woman smiled and said, "Well, now my question is gonna sound really dumb . . . So what chances do you guys think we have in the Utah 4th?"

She was scared of what the next election might mean for her future, but she came to that show believing that she had the power to help make it better. And because she and millions of others got to work – because we organized and volunteered and voted – a broader, more inclusive vision of democracy won. Not all at once. Not fully. Not finally. But it won. In 2018 it won. In 2020 it won. In 2022 it won. And no matter when you're reading this, democracy can win again.

Yes, this country is angry and anxious and fragmented. We've been through a pandemic, an insurrection, and a final season of *Game of Thrones* that completely fell apart. Everyone consumes their own media to fit their own biases. People seem to be getting in more fights on planes. The rent is too high, and the oceans are too warm, and the trains are too "not on the tracks." But for all the bluster and hostility and propaganda and money thrown at us to stop progress, to make us hate and fear one another, we have a not-so-secret weapon: the small-d democracy we can practice every day.

Václav Havel was a dissident and political prisoner in what was then Czechoslovakia, who agitated for democracy in his country for decades until he became its first democratically elected president. He talked about what it was like to fight for freedom when it wasn't clear if there was any chance of success. And here's what he said about the difference between expecting a better world and making one:

> Hope is definitely not the same thing as optimism. It is not the conviction that something will turn out well, but the certainty that something makes sense, regardless of how it turns out . . . It is also this hope, above all, which gives us the strength to live and continually to try new things, even in conditions that seem as hopeless as ours do, here and now.

As we've all seen, those who glom on to power will try to use hope against us. They'll flood our debates with enough lies that the truth becomes impossible to find. They'll argue that both sides are untrustworthy and all politicians are corrupt, that everyone cheats so you should too, that life is meant to be brutal and mean, that selfishness is natural and intolerance justified, that compassion is pathetic and mercy is weak. They want us to give up and turn inward. If democracy is our best weapon, cynicism is theirs. And as of this writing, it's a pretty even fight.

For too long, too many of us took democracy for granted. Not just in the sense that we didn't do enough (and we didn't do enough). But in how we assumed everyone understood why organizing our society in this way was so right and good. Maybe we'll look back on this era as a time of democratic backsliding, of acrimony and misinformation and crisis – when we realized that we no longer knew how to live together, or that social media showed us we never really knew how to live together in the first place.

Or maybe we'll look back on this time and say, "Wow, we really got off our asses."

We hope you enjoyed this guide, and if you didn't,
feel free to tweet any criticisms to @jonlovett.

SOURCES

In an effort to provide the most comprehensive and current guide possible, we consulted a variety of sources – from reputable news outlets to random TikToks that confirmed and reinforced our previously held opinions. Of the many resources that helped inform the text, honorable mention goes to surviving print media outlets, venerable nonprofits and research centers (looking at you, Pew!), and the various government websites that still mostly work. To get a better sense of where and how we gathered our ~~mis~~information, please refer back to Step 2 of this book, and to the media diet laid out by Favreau.

And while we don't want to play favorites, among the many sources that proved to be most useful were: the *New York Times*, the *Washington Post*, *FiveThirtyEight*, the *Atlanta Journal-Constitution*, NPR, CNN, Steve Bannon's *War Room* (just Tommy), the *Daily Beast*, *Politico*, and VOTESAVEAMERICA.COM.

In addition to our own experience, we drew on the wisdom of the many friends of the Pod whose quotes appear throughout the text, as well as the experts that we interviewed specifically for this book. It should be noted that some of the excerpts and blurbs were condensed and edited for the sake of clarity and stupid/reasonable grammar rules.

We are especially grateful for the contributions of our tireless researcher, Emily Zauzmer, whose attention to detail was truly remarkable. (She even listened to Ted Cruz's podcast just to confirm it actually exists.) Her thoughtfulness and thoroughness helped us to avoid calamity on more than one occasion and we so appreciate her passion for ~~politics~~ minutia.

As for the more specific data points mentioned:

"2008 Presidential Campaign Financial Activity Summarized: Receipts Nearly Double 2004 Total." Federal Election Commission, 8 June 2009.

"2020 Presidential Election Voting and Registration Tables Now Available." US Census Bureau, 29 Apr. 2021.

"2022 Voting and Registration Data Now Available." US Census Bureau, 2 May 2023.

Abernathy, Penelope Muse. "The State of Local News: The 2023 Report." Medill Local News Initiative, Northwestern University's Medill School of Journalism, Media, Integrated Marketing Communications, 16 Nov. 2023.

"Abortion Rights in the United States: NPR/PBS NewsHour/ Marist National Poll." Marist Poll, The Marist Institute for Public Opinion at Marist College, 26 Apr. 2023.

Agiesta, Jennifer, and Ariel Edwards-Levy. "CNN Poll: Percentage of Republicans Who Think Biden's 2020 Win Was Illegitimate Ticks Back Up Near 70%." CNN, 3 Aug. 2023.

"Al Smith Button." Heritage Auctions.

"Americans for More Rhombus." Federal Election Commission.

"Americans' Dismal Views of the Nation's Politics." Pew Research Center, 19 Sept. 2023.

"Anthony Weiner Covers and Headlines We're Particularly Proud Of." *New York Post*, 16 Sept. 2020.

"Audio and Podcasting Fact Sheet." Pew Research Center, 15 June 2023.

Balara, Victoria. "Fox News Poll: Voters Favor Gun Limits Over Arming Citizens to Reduce Gun Violence." Fox News, 27 Apr. 2023.

"Barack Obama (D)." OpenSecrets.

"Bearded Entrepreneurs for the Advancement of a Responsible Democracy." Federal Election Commission.

Beckel, Michael. "Outsized Influence." Issue One, 20 Apr. 2021.

Blake, Aaron. "How America Decided, at the Last Moment, to Elect Donald Trump." *Washington Post*, 17 Nov. 2016.

Caputo, Angela, et al. "After the Purge: How a Massive Voter Purge in Georgia Affected the 2018 Election." APM Reports, in collaboration with WABE, 29 Oct. 2019.

Cassidy, Christina A. "Far Too Little Vote Fraud to Tip Election to Trump, AP Finds." Associated Press, 14 Dec. 2021.

Chang, Alvin. "Why the Language on the Kansas Abortion Ballot Is So Confusing." *Guardian*, 2 Aug. 2022.

"Contacting Voters Works: Compiled Research." Grassroots Democrats HQ.

Corasaniti, Nick, and Allison McCann. "The 'Cost' of Voting in America: A Look at Where It's Easiest and Hardest." *New York Times*, 21 Sept. 2022.

"Democracy Index 2022." EIU, The Economist Intelligence Unit Limited, 2023.

"Did Money Win?" OpenSecrets.

Evers-Hillstrom, Karl. "Most Expensive Ever: 2020 Election Cost $14.4 Billion." OpenSecrets, 11 Feb. 2021.

"FACT SHEET: Treasury Department Releases First-of-Its-Kind Report on Benefits of Unions to the US Economy." US Department of the Treasury, 28 Aug. 2023.

Giorno, Taylor. "Democrats Anticipate Record-Shattering 2024 Presidential Bid for Joe Biden." OpenSecrets, 25 Apr. 2023.

Havel, Václav. Disturbing the Peace: A Conversation with Karel Hvížďala. 1991.

"Healthcare on the Ballot." Ballotpedia.

Huggins, Katherine. "Meet the 10 Biggest Megadonors for the 2022 Midterm Elections." MarketWatch, 11 Oct. 2022.

"The Infinite Dial 2023." Edison Research, with support from Amazon Music, Wondery, and ART19, 2023.

"Kentucky Senate 2020 Race." OpenSecrets.

Krupnikov, Yanna, and John Barry Ryan. "The Real Divide in America Is Between Political Junkies and Everyone Else." *New York Times*, 20 Oct. 2020.

"Marijuana Laws and Ballot Measures in the United States." Ballotpedia.

Massoglia, Anna, and Karl Evers-Hillstrom. "'Dark Money' Topped $1 Billion in 2020, Largely Boosting Democrats." OpenSecrets, 17 Mar. 2021.

McCarthy, Justin. "US Same-Sex Marriage Support Holds at 71% High." Gallup, Inc., 5 June 2023.

McDonald, Michael. "National Turnout Rates Graph." Election Lab, University of Florida.

Niesse, Mark. "Georgia Voter Registration Cancellations Conclude with 101K Removed." *Atlanta Journal-Constitution*, 17 Aug. 2021.

Nilsen, Ella, and Ariel Edwards-Levy. "CNN Poll: Large Majority of US Adults and Half of Republicans Agree with Biden's Goal to Slash Climate Pollution." CNN, 8 Dec. 2023.

Page, Susan, et al. "Exclusive: Support for Legal Abortion Rises a Year After Roe v. Wade Overturned – Poll." *USA TODAY*, 18 June 2023.

Pager, Tyler, and Michael Scherer. "Inside the Final Days Before Biden Announces His Reelection Bid." *Washington Post*, 22 Apr. 2023.

Perano, Ursula. "Video Shows Dr. Oz Saying He Has Two Houses. He Actually Has 10." The Daily Beast, 16 Aug. 2022.

"Presidential Job Approval Center." Gallup, Inc.

"Quick Facts: California." US Census Bureau.

"Quick Facts: Sheboygan City, Wisconsin." US Census Bureau.

"Quick Facts: Wyoming." US Census Bureau.

"Raptors for Jesus." Federal Election Commission.

Saad, Lydia. "Historically Low Faith in US Institutions Continues." Gallup, Inc., 6 July 2023.

Schraufnagel, Scot, et al. "Cost of Voting in the American States: 2022." *Election Law Journal: Rules, Politics, and Policy*, vol. 21, no. 3, 16 Sept. 2022.

"Sizing Up the Executive Branch: Fiscal Year 2017." US Office of Personnel Management, Feb. 2018.

"Social Media and News Fact Sheet." Pew Research Center, 15 Nov. 2023.

"Status of State Medicaid Expansion Decisions: Interactive Map." KFF.

"Stress in America: The State of Our Nation." American Psychological Association, 1 Nov. 2017.

"Top Spenders." OpenSecrets.

"Union Members – 2023." US Bureau of Labor Statistics, US Department of Labor, 23 Jan. 2024.

"US and World Population Clock." US Census Bureau.

Vandewalker, Ian. "Since Citizens United, a Decade of Super PACs." The Brennan Center for Justice, 14 Jan. 2020.

"Voter Purges." The Brennan Center for Justice.

Wasserman, David, et al. "2020 National Popular Vote Tracker." The Cook Political Report with Amy Walter.

Weiser, Wendy R., and Harold Ekeh. "The False Narrative of Vote-by-Mail Fraud." The Brennan Center for Justice, 10 Apr. 2020.

"The Youth Vote in 2022." CIRCLE, the Center for Information & Research on Civic Learning and Engagement, Tufts University's Jonathan M. Tisch College of Civic Life.

"Zombies of Tomorrow." Federal Election Commission.

For a more complete list of sources and citations, please contact our lawyer, Rudy Giuliani.

ABOUT THE AUTHORS

Former Obama White House aides **JON FAVREAU**, **JON LOVETT**, and **TOMMY VIETOR** are the hosts of the surprisingly popular podcast *Pod Save America*. A no-bullshit conversation about politics, *Pod Save America* cuts through the noise to break down the week's biggest and dumbest news, and helps listeners figure out what matters and how they can help. The hosts are regularly joined by journalists, activists, politicians, entertainers, and even world leaders, only some of whom regret their appearances.

JOSH HALLOWAY is an Emmy-nominated, WGA Award–winning writer and supervising producer for *Jimmy Kimmel Live*. He's also written multiple times for *The Oscars* and *The Primetime Emmys*.